ALSO FROM UK DRIVING SKILLS

Teaching a Learner Driver –
A guide for Amateur Instructors
Learning to Drive –
The Learner Driver's Manual
The Learner Driver's Logbook –
Lesson Plan & Progress Record
The Driving Test & How to Pass –
An Examiner's Guide to the 'L' Test

The Highway Code
How to Drive on a Motorway
Driving at Night & in Bad Weather

250 THEORY TEST QUESTIONS FOR:

Cars - Motorcycles - LGV - PCV - ADI

HIGHWAY CODE PLUS THEORY TEST QUESTIONS FOR:

Cars - Motorcycles - LGV - PCV - ADI

All available from www.ukdrivingskills.co.uk

250 THEORY TEST QUESTIONS FOR LGV

UK Driving Skills
Theory Test Question Series

Don L. Gates

www.ukdrivingskills.co.uk

Revised: 05/01/23

250 THEORY TEST QUESTIONS FOR LGV

This product includes the Driver and Vehicle Standards Agency (DVSA) revision question bank.

The Driver and Vehicle Standards Agency (DVSA) has given permission for the reproduction of Crown copyright material. DVSA does not accept responsibility for the accuracy of the reproduction.

Questions marked with an asterisk* are not from the DVSA question bank and are © Copyright UK Driving Skills

Contents

About the Theory Test

In order to take a theory test, you must have lived in England, Wales or Scotland for at least 185 days in the last 12 months before the day you sit your test. You need to obtain a provisional LGV driving licence before booking a test.

You must pass your theory test before you can take a practical driving test. The part 1 test is made up of 2 parts - multiple choice and hazard perception. You have to book both parts separately, but you can take them on the same day.

What to Take With You

You must take your UK photo card driving licence to your test. If you have a licence from Northern Ireland, take the photo card and paper counterpart licence. Your test will be cancelled and you will lose your fee if you do not take the correct things with you.

If you have an old style paper licence you must also take a valid passport for photo ID. If you do not have a passport, you need to get a photo card licence.

You will need to show your licence or ID to the staff when you arrive at the test centre. There will also be security checks to make sure that you're not carrying anything which could enable you to contact anyone outside of the test centre.

If you have any personal possessions, these must be placed in a secure locker or placed under your desk in a bag which will be given to you. It's best to take nothing with you that you don't really need.

Starting the Test

A member of staff will take you to a room where other candidates will be sat in cubicles also taking the test. You must be quiet but don't be afraid to ask questions.

The test is fairly straightforward and all the instructions will be shown on the screen in front of you. If you wish you can choose to have a practise session to get used to the way the test works.

Multiple Choice Questions

Once you begin the test, you will have 115 minutes to answer 100 questions. You need to score at least 85 points to pass.

In addition to this book, you can also use our online theory test practise pages to make sure that you're ready to pass at - https://www.ukdrivingskills.co.uk/theory-test-practise/

Hazard Perception

When you take the hazard perception element of the part 1 test, you should put on the provided headphones to watch an explanatory video.

You will be shown 19 video clips during which you need to click the mouse when you see a 'developing hazard', such as a vehicle about to emerge from a junction or a pedestrian about to step off the kerb; something which would cause you as a driver to alter speed or direction.

Click at the right time to score a maximum of 5 points for each clip. Don't just click randomly as you may be penalised for clicking too many times. One of the clips will have 2 hazards for you to identify. There is a maximum of 100 points and you need a minimum of 67 points to pass.

Test Result

You will get your test result shortly after finishing each test. You need to reach the minimum score in both parts to pass.

If you're not successful you must wait at least 3 working days before you can try again. When you've passed both parts, your theory test certificate will be posted to you. You need this when you book your Driver CPC part 3a and part 3b driving tests. The certificate is valid for 2 years. You need to pass the Driver CPC part 3a and part 3b driving tests within 2 years, otherwise you'll have to pass the part 1 theory test again.

Book a Theory Test

When you're ready to take a theory test, you can either:

- call the central booking line on 0300 200 11 22
- use the online booking system at - https://www.gov.uk/book-theory-test (easiest)

Before booking make sure that you have your:

- UK driving licence number
- an email address
- credit or debit card for payment

The current cost for the tests is £26 for the multiple choice exam and £11 for the hazard perception.

Special Needs

If you have any special needs you must mention this at the time of booking. Where possible, the theory test centre may be able to make adjustments to help you overcome any difficulties you may have.

About this Book

The material in this book is reproduced under licence from the Driver & Vehicle Standards Agency.

Questions are based on the official DVSA theory test question revision bank. They are designed to help you revise and practise for your theory test.

Questions marked with an asterisk* are not from the DVSA question bank and are © Copyright UK Driving Skills

Whilst every care is taken to ensure the accuracy of these questions and answers, if you do spot any errors please contact UK Driving Skills via our website to bring these to our attention.

About the Questions

Each practise set consists of 50 multiple choice questions. Mark the letter to the left of each answer you think is correct.

You will find the correct answers over the page; you will also be given an explanation of the answer helping to reinforce your knowledge on the subject.

Test One

Question 1

When would the driver of a car transporter need to be most aware of the front overhang of the trailer?

A   When overtaking

B   When turning

C   When loading

D   When braking

Question 2 *

What does this sign mean?

A   Traffic joining from the right

B   Lanes merge ahead

C   End of the dual-carriageway

D   Contraflow system in operation

Question 1

B - The long overhang at the front of a car transporter can cause problems where street furniture, such as lampposts and traffic signs, is sited close to junctions. Particular problems may be encountered when you're turning right and there are 'Keep left' bollards in the middle of the road you're turning into. Plan your route carefully to avoid such hazards.

Question 2

C - The dual-carriageway is coming to an end and you will be encountering oncoming traffic without a central divide. If you have been driving in the right hand lane you should move safely to the left in good time.

Question 3

What is the main reason for cleaning your wheels and tyres when you leave a building site?

A   To prevent mud from dropping onto the road

B   To keep the tyres in good condition

C   To prevent the tyres from damaging the road surface

D   To reduce air leakage from the tyre valves

Question 4

A group of horse riders comes towards you. What should you do if the leading rider's horse becomes nervous of your presence?

A   Increase speed to pass the riders quickly

B   Continue driving carefully and keep well to the left

C   Brake to a stop as quickly as possible

D   Brake gently to a stop until they have passed

Question 5

What should you do if you see a large box fall from a lorry onto the motorway?

A   Go to the next emergency telephone and report the hazard

B   Catch up with the lorry and try to get the driver's attention

C   Stop near to the box until the police arrive

D   Pull over to the hard shoulder, then remove the box

Answers

Question 3

A - If your wheels leave mud on the road, you must arrange for it to be cleared. A slippery, muddy surface could cause danger to other road users.

Question 4

D - If any animal you pass on the road becomes unsettled, you should brake gently to avoid startling them and come to a stop. A nervous animal is unpredictable, so you should wait until it has settled or passed by.

Question 5

A - Lorry drivers can be unaware of objects falling from their vehicles. If you see something fall onto a motorway, look to see if the driver pulls over. If they don't stop, don't attempt to retrieve the object yourself. Pull onto the hard shoulder near an emergency telephone and report the hazard.

Question 6

Which fuel provides a reduction in exhaust emissions harmful to human health?

A   Blue diesel

B   Red diesel

C   High-sulphur diesel

D   Low-sulphur diesel

Question 7

You are driving a lorry weighing more than 7.5 tonnes on a dual carriageway in England. What does this sign mean to you?

A   Maximum speed 40 mph

B   Maximum speed 70 mph

C   Maximum speed 50 mph

D   Maximum speed 60 mph

Question 6

D - Low-sulphur diesel reduces the levels of sulphur-dioxide particles in exhaust emissions. It's widely available and makes a contribution to reducing emissions that are harmful to human health.

Question 7

D - The maximum speed for lorries over 7.5 tonnes maximum authorised mass on a dual-carriageway is 60 mph (50 mph in Scotland). However, it may not always be appropriate or possible to drive at this speed, because of the weather, volume of traffic and other factors.

What does this sign mean?

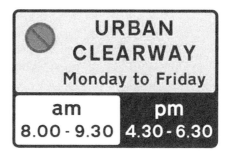

A You can park on the days and times shown

B No parking at all from Monday to Friday

C No parking on the days and times shown

D End of the urban clearway restrictions

You notice that one of your tyres has a bulge in the side wall. What will happen if you drive the vehicle?

A The vehicle will become unstable on corners

B Your speedometer will give an incorrect reading

C You'll break the law and risk prosecution

D Your tachograph reading won't be accurate

Answers

Question 8

C - Urban clearways are provided to keep traffic flowing at busy times. You may stop only briefly to set down or pick up passengers. Times of operation will vary from place to place, so always check the signs.

Question 9

C - It's a legal requirement that your tyres have at least the minimum permitted depth of tread and are in good condition before you start any journey. Make sure that you inspect them before setting off, and at regular intervals.

Question 10

What colour is the auxiliary line on a three-line braking system?

A   Yellow

B   Blue

C   Red

D   Green

Question 11

Your vehicle is more than 3 metres (9 feet 10 inches) high. Where is this information displayed?

A   In the driver's cab

B   On the weight plate

C   On the windscreen

D   In the engine bay

Question 12

What can a loose filler cap on your diesel fuel tank cause?

A   It can make the engine difficult to start

B   It can make the roads slippery for other road users

C   It can increase your vehicle's fuel consumption

D   It can increase the level of exhaust emissions

Answers

Question 10

B - If you're driving an articulated vehicle or a trailer combination, it's vital that you understand the rules that apply to coupling and uncoupling the brake lines. If you take a practical driving test with a trailer, you'll be expected to demonstrate this during the test. The lines are colour-coded: red is the emergency line, blue is the auxiliary line and yellow is the service line. They must be connected strictly in accordance with the correct procedure.

Question 11

A - It's a legal requirement that information about a vehicle's height can be seen by the driver from their seat. It's important to know the height of your vehicle so that you can avoid any height restrictions on your route.

Question 12

B - Diesel fuel can spill out if your filler cap isn't secured properly. This is most likely to occur on bends, junctions and roundabouts, where it will make the road slippery, especially if it's wet. At the end of a dry spell of weather, the road surfaces may have a high level of diesel spillage that hasn't been washed away by rain.

What does this sign mean?

A   The width of the road is 6 feet 6 inches (2 metres)

B   No vehicles over 6 feet 6 inches (2 metres) wide

C   No vehicles over 6 feet 6 inches (2 metres) high

D   Trailer length must not exceed 6 feet 6 inches (2 metres)

Where can a vehicle's axle weight limits be found?

A   On the operator's licence

B   On the weighbridge printout

C   On the vehicle plate

D   On the wheel rims

Question 13

B - You must always be aware of the size of your vehicle. Look out for road signs that show a width restriction. There should be an indication of this at the entrance to the road. Don't get into a situation where you have to reverse out of a narrow road because you haven't seen a sign.

Question 14

C - Individual axle weights are shown on the vehicle plate. This can be found in a prominent place on both the vehicle and trailer.

Question 15 *

You see a pedestrian approaching a zebra crossing. What should you normally do?

A   Accelerate before they step onto the crossing

B   Slow down and allow them to cross if they want to

C   Ignore them as they are still on the pavement

D   Stop and wave at them to cross the road

Question 16

Which of these should you do when driving in fog?

A   Use sidelights only to reduce dazzle

B   Switch on main beam headlights

C   Allow more time for your journey

D   Keep the vehicle ahead in sight

Question 17

What would you secure with a dog clip?

A   The air lines

B   The kingpin release handle

C   The parking brake

D   The diff-lock

Question 15

B - Pedestrians have right of way once they step onto the crossing, but you should always slow down and be ready to stop to allow them to step out. Never wave them on, they could step into another danger they have not seen.

Question 16

C - If you have to travel and someone is expecting you at the other end, let them know that you'll be taking longer than usual for your journey. This will stop them worrying if you don't turn up on time and will also take the pressure off you, so you don't feel you have to rush.

Question 17

B - When recoupling, you must connect the dog clip to secure the kingpin release handle.

Question 18

What is prohibited when a Red Route is in operation?

A   Changing lanes

B   Overtaking

C   Stopping or parking

D   Driving at more than 20 mph

Question 19 *

You see some elderly and slow moving people starting to cross the road ahead of you. What should you do?

A   Wave them to continue so they know it is safe

B   Slow down and give them time to cross

C   Go wide and drive around them

D   Warn them of your approach by tapping the horn

Question 20

You have broken down at night on a two-way road. How should you try to leave the vehicle?

A   Partly on the pavement

B   On a grass verge

C   On the right of the road

D   On the left of the road

Answers

Question 18

C - The hours of operation of Red Routes vary from one area to another. As a rule, you mustn't stop on a Red Route, but there may be special marked boxes where loading and unloading can be carried out at certain times. Look out for signs giving information about the restrictions in place.

Question 19

B - Elderly people may have impaired judgement, they may not realise what speed you are doing, and they may be slow to cross the road. You need to be patient and considerate. You should never wave people to cross, they may step into a danger that you haven't seen.

Question 20

D - If your vehicle breaks down, try to stop on the left, facing in the same direction as the flow of traffic. This will help other drivers to see you, as your red reflectors will show to the rear. Don't stop on the pavement, as the weight of the vehicle may damage paving stones and underground services.

Question 21

You are driving between the hours of 11.30 pm and 7.00 am. When must you switch off your vehicle's reverse warning bleeper?

A   Before reversing on a road that has a temporary speed limit

B   Before reversing on a road that has a 30 mph speed limit

C   Before reversing on a road that has the national speed limit

D   Before reversing on a road that has a 40 mph speed limit

Question 22

When are air deflectors most effective?

A   When there is a side wind

B   When there's a strong tailwind

C   When reversing into wind

D   When there is a headwind

Question 23 *

Pedestrians have just cleared the road at a puffin crossing. What signal will you see next?

A   Green

B   Flashing amber

C   Red & amber

D   Flashing green

Answers

Question 21

B - Your vehicle will make more noise than a car, so you should try to avoid making unnecessary noise at any time of the day or night. This is especially important when you're in a residential area at a time when people are likely to be sleeping.

Question 22

D - Air deflectors reduce wind resistance by streamlining the vehicle. They're most effective when there's a headwind. The streamlining also reduces the vehicle's fuel consumption.

Question 23

C - Puffin crossings have infra-red sensors that detect when pedestrians are crossing and hold the red traffic signal until the crossing is clear. The use of a sensor means there's no flashing amber phase as there is with a pelican crossing and they will instead show the normal traffic light sequence.

Question 24

Your vehicle has collided with a railway bridge. What information must you give the railway authority when you telephone them?

A   The bridge number

B   The height of your vehicle

C   The make and model of your vehicle

D   The type of bridge

Question 25

During periods of illness, your ability to drive may be impaired. What must you do?

A   See your doctor each time before you drive

B   Take smaller doses of any medicines

C   Make sure you're medically fit to drive

D   Take all your medicines with you when you drive

Question 26

You're turning right onto a dual carriageway. What should you do before emerging?

A   Stop, apply the handbrake and then select a low gear

B   Position your vehicle well to the left of the side road

C   Check that the central reservation is wide enough for your vehicle

D   Make sure that you leave enough room for a vehicle behind

Answers

Question 24

A - The railway authority needs to know immediately if one of their bridges has been hit. You'll need to tell them the number of the bridge so they can identify it. The railway authority will then take action to prevent railway passengers from being put at risk.

Question 25

C - Only drive if you're fit to do so. Driving when you're ill or taking some medicines can affect your concentration and judgement. It may also cause you to become drowsy or even fall asleep.

Question 26

C - Before emerging right onto a dual carriageway, make sure that the central reservation is deep enough to protect your vehicle. If it isn't, you should treat the dual carriageway as one road and check that it's clear in both directions before pulling out. Neglecting to do this could place part or all of your vehicle in the path of approaching traffic and cause a collision.

Question 27

What does this sign mean?

A   Give way to oncoming vehicles

B   Approaching traffic passes you on both sides

C   Turn off at the next available junction

D   Pass on either side

Question 28 *

What is the purpose of the yellow road markings in this picture?

A   To protect drivers who are turning right

B   To guide you into the correct position

C   To keep an area clear at a junction

D   To show an area reserved for emergency vehicles

Question 27

D - These signs are seen in one-way streets that have more than one lane. When you see this sign, use the route that's the most convenient and doesn't require a late change of direction.

Question 28

C - Yellow box junctions are marked on the road to prevent the road becoming blocked. Don't enter the box unless your exit road is clear. You may wait in the box if you want to turn right and your exit road is clear but oncoming traffic or other vehicles waiting to turn right are preventing you from making the turn.

Question 29

You've had a breakdown on the hard shoulder of a motorway. When the problem has been fixed, how should you rejoin the main carriageway?

A   Move out onto the carriageway, then build up your speed

B   Move out onto the carriageway using your hazard warning lights

C   Gain speed on the hard shoulder before moving out onto the carriageway

D   Signal, but wait on the hard shoulder until someone flashes their lights at you

Question 30

A driver is convicted of bringing illegal immigrants into the UK. How is the fine calculated?

A   For each court attendance they make

B   For each person they bring in

C   For each country the immigrants are from

D   For each family group they bring in

Answers

Question 29

C - Signal your intention and build up sufficient speed on the hard shoulder so that you can filter into a safe gap in the traffic. Don't push your way in, causing other traffic to alter speed or direction.

Question 30

B - If convicted, the current fine for each illegal immigrant brought into the UK is £2000. This fine can be imposed on each responsible person; this includes the vehicle driver, owner and hirer.

Question 31

What must you do at this junction?

A   Stop behind the line, then edge forward to see clearly

B   Stop beyond the line, at a point where you can see clearly

C   Stop only if there is traffic on the main road

D   Stop only if you are turning to the left

Question 32

You're on a motorway at night. In which situation may you have your headlights switched off?

A   When there are vehicles close in front of you

B   When you are travelling below 50 mph

C   When the motorway is brightly lit

D   When your vehicle is broken down on the hard shoulder

Question 31

A - The 'stop' sign has been put here because the view into the main road is poor. You must stop because it won't be possible to take proper observation while you're moving.

Question 32

D - Always use your headlights at night on a motorway, unless you've had to stop on the hard shoulder. If you have to use the hard shoulder, switch off your headlights but leave your parking lights on, so that your vehicle can be seen by other road users.

Question 33

You are driving a lorry with a sleeper cab. When would a quick sideways glance be helpful?

A   Before signalling to stop

B   Before climbing a steep hill

C   When traffic is merging from the right or left

D   When driving round sharp bends

Question 34

You are delivering boxes of chilled food to a supermarket. What specific training would you need?

A   Hygiene procedures

B   ADR procedures

C   Waste-handling procedures

D   Ecosafe driving procedures

Answers

Question 33

C - The size and design of some cabs can create blind spots. This is especially true of a sleeper cab. A quick sideways glance might show something you can't see in your mirrors, especially when traffic is merging.

Question 34

A - Chilled foods are transported at temperatures above freezing point. Drivers need to be trained in hygiene procedures and how to operate refrigeration units.

Question 35

What should you do if the load on your lorry becomes insecure?

A   Continue at a slower speed to ensure the load doesn't fall off

B   Attach 'hazard' boards to the load to warn other road users

C   Park and re-secure the load before continuing

D   Inform base at the earliest opportunity

Question 36

On a road where trams operate, which of these vehicles will be most at risk from the tram rails?

A   Cars

B   Cycles

C   Buses

D   Lorries

Question 35

C - If you become aware that any part of your load is insecure, you must stop as soon as it's safe to do so. Re-secure the load before continuing your journey. If this isn't possible, then you must seek assistance. Don't take risks.

Question 36

B - The narrow wheels of a bicycle can become stuck in the tram rails, causing the cyclist to stop suddenly, wobble or even lose balance altogether. The tram lines are also slippery, which could cause a cyclist to slide or fall off. Make sure that you allow riders plenty of room in these situations.

Question 37

Where does a high-pressure fuel injector deliver fuel?

A   Into the combustion chamber

B   Into the carburettors

C   Into the crankcase

D   Into the manifold

Question 38 *

How does a toucan crossing differ from other types of crossing?

A   Horse riders can also use it

B   Traffic wardens control it

C   It only operates at peak times

D   Cyclists can also use it

Question 39

Where can you find reflective amber studs on a motorway?

A   Separating the slip road from the motorway

B   On the left-hand edge of the road

C   On the right-hand edge of the road

D   Separating the lanes

Question 37

A - Most diesel engines use a high-pressure fuel-injector system that will deliver pressurised fuel directly into the combustion chamber of the engine. This system is known as a direct-injection engine.

Question 38

D - Toucan crossings are shared by pedestrians and cyclists, who are allowed to ride across. Unlike the pelican crossing there is no flashing amber phase, the light sequence is the same as normal traffic lights.

Question 39

C - At night or in poor visibility, reflective studs on the road help you to judge your position on the carriageway. Amber studs mark the edge of the central reservation.

You are loading goods of varying weights. How should they be distributed over the width of the vehicle?

A   Heavy items at the front, light items at the rear

B   Heavy items near the centre line, light items towards the sides

C   Light items at the front, heavy items at the rear

D   Light items near the centre line, heavy items towards the side

Question 41

Which sign means that there may be people walking along the road?

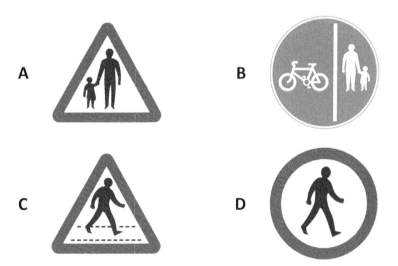

A

B

C

D

Answers

Question 40

B - To achieve maximum stability, the load should be placed to keep the centre of gravity as low as possible. To do this, heavy items should be placed close to the centre line and spread over the full length of the vehicle. Lighter items should be placed along the sides.

Question 41

A - Always check the road signs. Triangular signs are warning signs: they inform you about hazards ahead and help you to anticipate any problems. There are a number of different signs showing pedestrians. Learn the meaning of each one.

Question 42

Before starting a journey, you want to check your brake-system warning lights. What can you do when these aren't operated by the ignition switch?

A   Get someone behind to check your brake lights

B   Check them at the end of your journey

C   Look for a check switch on the dashboard

D   Pump the brake pedal a number of times

Question 43 *

If you overload an axle while loading your lorry, what could this cause?

A   Errors in the tachograph readings

B   Damage to the road

C   Excessive oil usage

D   Excessive spray in wet weather

Question 44 *

What step can you take to reduce environmental pollution?

A   Make use of town and city bypasses

B   Make regular use of the air conditioning

C   Use red diesel instead of regular fuel

D   Use lower gears for longer periods

Question 42

C - A warning-lights check is sometimes performed automatically when the ignition is switched on. However, you may need to do this manually by operating a separate check switch. Never start a journey without carrying out this check. If there's a problem, have it repaired before you set off.

Question 43

B - You could be fined and given penalty points on your licence if you overload an axle, as the force this creates on the road could result in damage to the surface as well as underground services.

Question 44

A - By using bypasses you are much more likely to be able maintain a steady speed rather than getting stuck in the stop-start traffic of busy city centres. Driving at a steady speed will use much less fuel.

Question 45

What would staff from HM Revenue and Customs (HMRC) be looking for at a roadside check?

A   Red diesel

B   Drivers' hours records

C   Exhaust emissions

D   Vehicle defects

Question 46

When is a buffer lane most likely to be in use?

A   When it is windy

B   When going uphill

C   When it is foggy

D   When it is icy

Question 47

What should you do if you lose your way in heavy traffic?

A   Stop at traffic lights and ask pedestrians

B   Shout to other drivers to ask them the way

C   Drive on until you find a safe place to stop

D   Check a map as you keep moving with the traffic

Answers

Question 45

A - HMRC can check the type of fuel you're using, and the type and legality of your load. Red diesel is dyed gas oil with a lower tax than regular diesel. It can only be used in agricultural and construction vehicles (such as tractors). Red diesel mustn't be used in freight transport.

Question 46

A - A buffer lane is used when the wind begins to cause a risk to high-sided vehicles. At other times, it will be a normal lane. Don't use the buffer lane unless your vehicle has been blown off course into the lane, or you need to use it to avoid an incident or collision.

Question 47

C - Driving in heavy traffic needs 100% concentration. If you become lost, find a safe place to stop before checking a map or asking for directions. Don't risk losing concentration by glancing at a map while driving, even if you're in traffic that keeps stopping.

Question 48

What should you do before driving your lorry away from a wet construction site at the side of a motorway?

A   Hose down the wheels

B   Turn on your amber beacon

C   Drain the air tanks

D   Set your tachograph to 'other work'

Question 49

You are driving in traffic at the speed limit for the road. What should you do if the driver behind is trying to overtake?

A   Move closer to the car ahead, so the driver behind has no room to overtake

B   Wave the driver behind to overtake when it's safe

C   Keep a steady course and allow the driver behind to overtake

D   Accelerate to get away from the other driver

Question 50

You are about to start a long journey midway through the day. What should you do if you notice that the sidelights work but the headlights are faulty?

A   Don't drive until they are repaired

B   Drive only until light begins to fade

C   Avoid driving on motorways after dark

D   Drive only if the weather is good

Answers

Question 48

A - Before leaving a construction site, check your vehicle for mud and for debris wedged between double rear wheels. It's important that you prevent any mud or debris from being deposited on the road, where it could be a danger to other road users.

Question 49

C - Keep a steady course to give the driver behind an opportunity to overtake safely. If necessary, slow down. Reacting incorrectly to another driver's impatience can lead to danger.

Question 50

A - To comply with the law, all lights must be in good working order, even in daylight when they are not being used. Before you set out, make sure that everything is working and get any faulty lights fixed. You may need to use your headlights or other lights if you are delayed or find yourself driving in conditions of reduced visibility.

2022

The Highway Code

The Rules of the Road

UK Driving Skills
www.ukdrivingskills.co.uk

Test Two

Question 1

You are coming up to a roundabout. A cyclist on your left is signalling to turn right. What should you do?

A   Overtake wide on the right

B   Give a warning with your horn

C   Signal the cyclist to move across

D   Stay behind the cyclist

Question 2

You are uncoupling a trailer. What must you do before disconnecting any of the air lines?

A   Apply the trailer parking brake

B   Disconnect the electrical line

C   Drain the air tanks

D   Lower the landing gear

Question 3 *

When following another vehicle, why should you not follow it too closely?

A   There will be too much turbulence

B   Your engine will be starved of air

C   Your view will be restricted

D   Your sat nav may lose its signal

Answers

Question 1

D - If you're following a cyclist who's signalling to turn right at a roundabout, stay behind and leave plenty of room.

Although it may not be considered safe by many, the Highway Code states that cyclists may turn right using the left-hand lane; you need to be aware that the rider may cross your path as you approach your exit.

Question 2

A - Whenever you uncouple a trailer, you must work through the uncoupling process methodically. Start by making sure that the brakes are applied on both the vehicle and the trailer.

Question 3

C - The closer you get the rear of another vehicle the less you will be able to see past it. This will limit your ability to react in time to hazards in addition to giving you less distance in which to stop.

Question 4

You're in a tunnel and you see this sign. What does it mean?

A Beware of pedestrians: no footpath ahead

B Direction to emergency pedestrian exit

C No access for pedestrians

D Beware of pedestrians crossing ahead

Question 5

What could prevent air pressure from building up in an air-brake system in very cold weather?

A Moisture in the air may form bubbles in the brake fluid

B The air will contract, reducing the pressure

C Moisture drawn in with the air may freeze and cause a blockage

D The dampness may cause valves to rust

Answers

Question 4

B - If you have to leave your vehicle and get out of a tunnel by an emergency exit, do so as quickly as you can. Follow the signs directing you to the nearest exit point. If there are several people using the exit, don't panic but try to leave in a calm and orderly manner.

Question 5

C - When air is compressed, moisture condenses and collects in the air tanks. This can find its way along the network of pipes connected to the brakes. In frosty weather, the moisture can freeze in the pipes, blocking them completely. On modern vehicles, the air is dried before it's compressed and the air tanks drain automatically to shed any moisture. On older vehicles, the air tanks need draining manually.

Question 6

Why are brushes often fitted to a large vehicle's wheel arch?

A   To prevent snow from building up behind the wheel

B   To remove objects from the tyre tread

C   To reduce spray on wet roads

D   To clear mud from the tyres on building sites

Question 7

What does this sign mean?

A   Slippery road

B   Double bend

C   Cable laying ahead

D   Overhead electrified cable

Answers

Question 6

C - The brushes are part of a spray-suppression system. They reduce the amount of water thrown up at the sides and rear of the vehicle. Check them regularly for security. If they become worn, make sure they're replaced.

Question 7

D - It's essential to know the height of your vehicle before setting off. This should be clearly marked, usually in the cab, and visible from the driving position. Look out for restrictions that you may not have seen on a map – they may be temporary.

Question 8

Traffic signs giving orders are generally which shape?

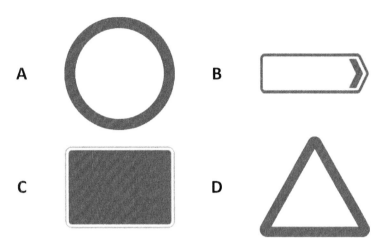

A

B

C

D

Question 9

You've been driving non-stop since 5.00 am. The time is now 9.30 am. Under EU rules, what length of break must you take?

A   At least 15 minutes

B   At least 30 minutes

C   At least 45 minutes

D   At least 60 minutes

Question 8

A - Road signs in the shape of a circle give orders. Those with a red circle are mostly prohibitive. Signs giving orders must always be obeyed.

Question 9

C - You must take an uninterrupted break of 45 minutes after four-and-a-half hours of driving. This break may be replaced by two shorter breaks of at least 15 and 30 minutes, taken in that order, during the four-and-a-half hours. During any break, you mustn't drive or do any other work.

Question 10

Why are ropes unsuitable to tie down a load of scrap metal?

A   Ropes are hard to tie

B   Ropes can wear and snap

C   Ropes will loosen in rain

D   Ropes are hard to untie

Question 11

You're driving a long vehicle. When might you sometimes need to straddle lanes?

A   When turning at tight junctions

B   When driving on motorways

C   When coming to contraflow systems

D   When you're not sure which way to go

Question 12

Which load may need to be transported at a controlled temperature?

A   Sugar

B   Chemicals

C   Beer barrels

D   Bulk grain

Answers

Question 10

B - When securing a load, the driver must use the most suitable type of restraint. Scrap metal is likely to have sharp edges that could wear through straps or ropes. Security of the load is the driver's responsibility; a load that has been correctly secured shouldn't move if an emergency arises.

Question 11

A - When driving a long vehicle around corners, it's sometimes necessary to adopt a different road position to avoid mounting the kerb or colliding with street furniture such as lampposts or traffic signs. Other road users may not understand what you intend to do next. Watch them carefully and always signal in good time.

Question 12

B - Some highly dangerous chemicals have to be transported at prescribed temperatures. Drivers must be fully trained in the use of these specially designed, temperature-controlled vehicles.

Question 13

What do heated fuel lines prevent?

A   The cab temperature dropping

B   The radiator from freezing

C   The windows from misting

D   The diesel from partly solidifying

Question 14

When should you use a crawler lane?

A   When turning right from a major road

B   When parking to have a rest

C   When slowing down for a motorway exit

D   When letting faster traffic overtake you

Question 15

You're driving through a tunnel and the traffic is flowing normally. Which lights should you use?

A   Side lights

B   Front spot lights

C   Dipped headlights

D   No lights are necessary

Question 13

D - In cold weather, diesel fuel can solidify as it starts to freeze. This is known as waxing. Waxing prevents the fuel from flowing properly and this can stop the engine from running.

Question 14

D - Many vehicles are very powerful and can maintain speed even when climbing a gradient. Even if your vehicle is capable of maintaining speed, you can still use the crawler lane to make it easier for other road users to overtake safely.

Question 15

C - Before entering a tunnel, you should switch on your dipped headlights, as this will allow you to see and be seen. In many tunnels, it's a legal requirement. Don't wear sunglasses while driving in a tunnel. You may wish to tune your radio to a local channel for traffic information.

Question 16

A vehicle has rolled over and caught fire. The driver's hands and arms have been burned. How could you help the driver?

A   Remove smouldering clothing

B   Try to put out the fire

C   Remove anything sticking to the burns

D   Douse the burns with cool water

Question 17

How frequently should the components of a fifth-wheel coupling be inspected?

A   Monthly

B   Daily

C   Weekly

D   Yearly

Question 18

You are turning left into a side road. What hazard should you be especially aware of?

A   A change in speed limit

B   Pedestrians

C   Traffic congestion

D   Parked vehicles

Question 16

D - Don't remove anything sticking to a burn. You may cause further damage and introduce infection into the wound. If you can, douse the burn with clean, cool water for at least 10 minutes if possible.

Question 17

A - A fifth wheel must be maintained properly. It requires regular lubrication and inspection. This should be carried out monthly or every 10 000 km – whichever comes first.

Question 18

B - Look into the road before you turn and always give way to any pedestrians who are crossing or waiting to step out.

Question 19

What does this warning light on the instrument panel mean?

A   Low fuel pressure

B   Low oil pressure

C   Low water pressure

D   Low coolant level

Question 20

What should you do if a trailer starts to swing from side to side while you're towing it?

A   Let go of the steering wheel and let it correct itself

B   Steer in the direction the trailer is swinging

C   Accelerate gradually until it stabilises

D   Ease off the accelerator to reduce your speed

Answers

Question 19

B - You should be familiar with all the warning lights fitted to your vehicle. The oil warning light indicates low oil pressure or lack of oil. If it lights up, report the fault and don't continue until it's been corrected.

Question 20

D - Strong winds or buffeting from large vehicles can cause a trailer or caravan to swing from side to side ('snake'). If this happens, ease off the accelerator. Don't brake, steer sharply or increase your speed.

Question 21

Which symbol on your tachograph shows your break/rest period?

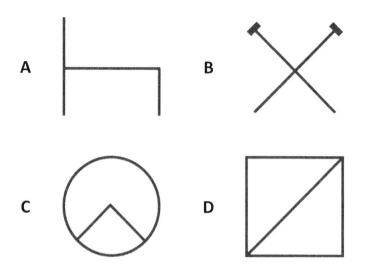

A

B

C

D

Question 22

How would you identify a section of road used by trams?

A   There would be a different surface texture

B   There would be metal studs around it

C   There would be zigzag markings alongside it

D   There would be yellow hatch markings around it

Question 21

A - A tachograph allows you to select the mode or task that you're undertaking. Time spent on that task is then recorded automatically. Each task has a different symbol. You need to know the meaning of each, so that your records are correct. The modes are: driving, doing other work, on duty and available for work, and taking a break or rest.

Question 22

A - Trams may run on roads used by other vehicles and pedestrians. The section of road used by trams is known as the reserved area and should be kept clear. It usually has a different surface, edged with white lane markings.

Question 23

What does this traffic sign mean?

A   Hump bridge

B   Humps in the road

C   Steep camber

D   Soft verges

Question 24

Which symbol on a lorry shows its load is dangerous when wet?

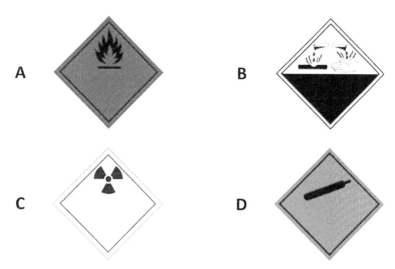

Question 23

B - These humps have been put in place to slow the traffic down. They're usually found in residential areas. Slow down to an appropriate speed.

Question 24

A - If any vehicle displaying a warning symbol is involved in an incident, the consequences could be serious. The emergency services need to be aware of how a dangerous or hazardous material will behave in different situations; for example, when it's wet.

Question 25

You have to drive onto a muddy building site. Why should you switch on your diff-lock?

A   To make your steering lighter

B   To improve your fuel consumption

C   To increase your engine power

D   To make the wheels less likely to spin

Question 26 *

What does this red cross on a blue background mean?

A   No waiting

B   No stopping

C   No entry

D   No vehicles

Question 25

D - Engaging the diff-lock means that the driven wheels are locked together. This reduces the likelihood of wheel spin. Remember to switch off the diff-lock as soon as you're on firm ground again, otherwise you could damage the transmission.

Question 26

B - The sign indicates that the road is a 'clearway' where no stopping is allowed. There may also be an information plate telling you what times this restriction is in force. If there is no time plate, you should assume that the clearway is in operation 24 hours.

Your lorry has a double-deck body. The top tier is loaded and the lower deck is empty. When will the vehicle be most at risk of overturning?

A   In heavy rain

B   When you are braking

C   When you are accelerating

D   In high winds

What does this arrow marking in the middle of the road mean?

A   Traffic should use the hard shoulder

B   The road is about to bend to the left

C   Overtaking drivers should move back to the left

D   It is a safe place to overtake

Question 27

D - A lorry loaded like this will be top-heavy and more likely to overturn in high winds or when cornering. If you're only carrying half a load, you should try to carry it on the lower deck.

Question 28

C - The white arrow warns any overtaking drivers that they should move back to the left. There is probably a hazard ahead such as a dip in the road, a bend, or a traffic island.

Question 29

You take some cough medicine given to you by a friend. What should you do before driving?

A   Ask your friend if taking the medicine affected their driving

B   Drink some strong coffee one hour before driving

C   Check the label to see if the medicine will affect your driving

D   Drive a short distance to see if the medicine is affecting you

Question 30

How many days does a driver's smart card normally cover?

A   7

B   14

C   21

D   28

Question 31

What colour are the reflective studs between a motorway and its slip road?

A   Amber

B   White

C   Green

D   Red

Question 29

C - If you've taken medicine, never drive without first checking what the side effects might be; they might affect your judgement and perception, and therefore endanger lives.

Question 30

D - The smart card will record information covering a period of about 28 days. If you use it beyond this period, some of the recorded information will be overwritten.

Question 31

C - The studs between the carriageway and the hard shoulder are normally red. These change to green where there's a slip road, helping you to identify slip roads when visibility is poor or when it's dark.

Question 32

How often must an analogue tachograph be checked?

A Every year

B Every two years

C Every five years

D Every six years

Question 33

What might happen if using the brakes continuously causes them to overheat?

A The brake pedal will become stiff

B The brakes will be less effective

C The air pressure will increase

D The brakes will work better

Question 32

B - An analogue tachograph must be checked every two years and recalibrated and sealed every six years. This must be done at an approved calibration centre. Digital tachographs, unlike analogue ones, must be recalibrated every two years.

Question 33

B - Whenever you brake, the brakes convert the moving energy of your vehicle into heat. Continuous use of the brakes, particularly from high speed or on long steep descents, can cause the shoes and drums to overheat. This will make them less effective and, in some cases, they may not work at all.

What should you do when approaching traffic lights where red and amber are showing together?

A Drive on if the way is clear

B Start to edge over the stop line

C Wait for the green light

D Start to pick up speed

You are the first to arrive at the scene of a serious incident. What should you do?

A Leave as soon as another motorist arrives

B Flag down other motorists to help you

C Drag all casualties away from the vehicles

D Call the emergency services promptly

Question 34

C - You should not cross the line until the green light shows. Where the lights have just changed, be aware that other traffic may still be crossing and always look to make sure that your way is clear.

Question 35

D - At a crash scene you can help in practical ways, even if you aren't trained in first aid. Call the emergency services and make sure you don't put yourself or anyone else in danger. The safest way to warn other traffic is by switching on your hazard warning lights.

Question 36

What should you do if your anti-lock brake (ABS) warning light stays on?

A   Check the brake-fluid level

B   Check the footbrake free play

C   Make sure this is corrected at your next service

D   Have the brakes checked as soon as possible

Question 37 *

What's the meaning of this sign?

A   No vehicles over height shown

B   No vehicles over width shown

C   Lane only available for vehicles over height shown

D   Lane only available for vehicles over width shown

Answers

Question 36

D - Consult the vehicle handbook or a garage before driving the vehicle any further. Only drive to a garage if it's safe to do so. If you aren't sure, get expert help.

Question 37

A - You must always be aware of the height of the vehicle you are driving; there will be a notice inside the cab as a reminder. You must also be aware that your vehicle height may be increased beyond this by the type of load you are carrying.

Question 38

What is a rumble device designed to do?

A   Reduce noise levels

B   Prevent cattle escaping

C   Alert you to a hazard

D   Alert you to low tyre pressure

Question 39

You're driving towards this left-hand bend. What danger should you be most aware of?

A   A change in speed limit

B   No white lines in the centre of the road

C   No sign to warn you of the bend

D   Pedestrians walking towards you

Question 38

C - A rumble device consists of raised markings or strips across the road, designed to give drivers and riders an audible, visual and tactile warning. These devices are used in various locations, including in the line separating the hard shoulder and the left-hand lane on the motorway and on the approach to some hazards.

Question 39

D - Pedestrians walking on a road with no pavement should walk against the direction of the traffic. You can't see around this bend: there may be hidden dangers. Always keep this in mind and give yourself time to react if a hazard does appear.

A coach is overtaking you. What should you do when it is safe for the driver to move back to the left?

A   Flash your headlights twice

B   Switch your sidelights on and off

C   Flash your headlights once

D   Do nothing and let the driver decide

What can result from overloading an axle?

A   Reduced braking efficiency

B   Reduced braking distance

C   Increased kerbside weight

D   Increased engine temperature

Question 40

D - When you're being overtaken, the other driver has to decide when it's safe to complete the manoeuvre. Don't give an unofficial signal, however well intended. There may be a hazard you're unable to see from your position.

Question 41

A - Too much weight on an axle can reduce braking efficiency and cause brake fade. As well as being dangerous, exceeding the axle weight limit is an offence that can result in prosecution.

Question 42

What does this sign mean?

A   End of two-way road

B   Give priority to vehicles coming towards you

C   You have priority over vehicles coming towards you

D   Start of two-way road

Question 43

What effect will continuous use of the air-conditioning system have on fuel consumption?

A   Increase it by about 15 per cent

B   Increase it by about 30 per cent

C   Increase it by about 50 per cent

D   Increase it by about 75 per cent

Question 42

C - You may have priority but don't force your way through. Show courtesy and consideration to other road users. Even though you have priority, make sure oncoming traffic is going to give way before you continue.

Question 43

A - Avoid using air-conditioning systems for long periods, as they can increase fuel consumption by about 15%. Try to drive with fuel economy and the environment in mind.

Question 44

You are approaching a bridge that has no height restriction on it. What will be the minimum height under the bridge?

A   3.6 metres [11 feet 10 inches]

B   4.4 metres [14 feet 5 inches]

C   4.8 metres [16 feet]

D   5 metres [16 feet 6 inches]

Question 45

You are securing a load using ropes. What is the minimum diameter of rope that you should use?

A   5 mm

B   10 mm

C   15 mm

D   20 mm

Question 46

How can you use your vehicle's engine to control your speed?

A   By changing to a lower gear

B   By selecting reverse gear

C   By changing to a higher gear

D   By selecting neutral

Answers

Question 44

D - The headroom under bridges in the UK is at least 5 metres (16 feet 6 inches), unless otherwise stated. Where the overhead clearance is arched, this headroom is normally only between the limits marked.

Question 45

B - When using ropes, the ends should be spliced or otherwise treated to prevent fraying. The rope should be of at least three-strand construction, with a normal diameter of at least 10 mm.

Question 46

A - You should brake and slow down before selecting a lower gear. The gear can then be used to keep the speed low and help you control the vehicle. This is particularly helpful on long downhill stretches, where brake fade can occur if the brakes overheat.

Question 47

You are driving down a snow-covered hill. Why should you take care when using an independent endurance brake (retarder)?

A   Compressed air could escape

B   Your speed could increase

C   The drive-wheels could lock

D   Your brakes could overheat

Question 48 *

There is a puffin crossing ahead. Pedestrians are crossing and your light is red. When will the lights change?

A   When sensors pick up that vehicles are approaching

B   After pedestrians have finished crossing

C   When someone presses the button on the other side

D   The lights will change after a set period of time

Question 49 *

When should you consider the effect a speed limiter will have on your vehicle?

A   When first moving off

B   When going downhill

C   When going uphill

D   When overtaking

Answers

Question 47

C - Select an appropriate gear in good time and, if your vehicle has a dashboard-mounted lever, apply the endurance brake (retarder) in stages. Braking too much, too soon may result in locking your drive wheels.

Question 48

B - Puffin crossings are controlled by sensors which follow the movement of pedestrians. The lights will only change when people have safely reached the other side.

Question 49

D - Overtaking must be carefully planned. Make sure that you have enough speed in reserve before you pull out to ensure that you can get safely past the other vehicle before your speed limiter cuts in.

Question 50 *

What should you do when you see an emergency vehicle behind you?

A   Move aside and slow down when it is safe

B   Continue normally and let them decide when to pass

C   Maintain your speed but signal left to let them know they can pass

D   Brake to an immediate stop until they pass

Question 50

A - You should do what you can to let the emergency vehicle pass, but do not suddenly stop as this could take others by surprise and cause danger in itself. Reduce speed and move over to the left as soon as it is safe to do so.

2022

The Highway Code

& LGV Theory Test Practise Questions

Includes 200 interactive practise questions

UK Driving Skills

Test Three

Question 1

At a junction, you see this sign partly covered by snow. What does it mean?

A Crossroads

B Give way

C Stop

D No entry

Question 2

A casualty isn't breathing normally and needs CPR. At what rate should you press down and release on the centre of their chest?

A 10 per minute

B 60 per minute

C 120 per minute

D 240 per minute

Answers

Question 1

C - The 'stop' sign is the only road sign that's octagonal. This is so that it can be recognised and obeyed even if it's obscured (for example, by snow).

Question 2

C - If a casualty isn't breathing normally, cardiopulmonary resuscitation (CPR) may be needed to maintain circulation. Place two hands on the centre of the chest and press down hard and fast, around 5– 6 centimetres and about twice a second.

Question 3

You are travelling along a motorway. When are you allowed to overtake on the left?

A   If you're within one mile of your exit

B   If the driver ahead won't move over to let you pass

C   If you're in stationary traffic but the hard shoulder is clear

D   If you're driving in a slow-moving traffic queue

Question 4 *

What can you do to prevent fuel spillage?

A   Close and secure the filler cap

B   Place the drip tray correctly

C   Stop refuelling when the tank is half full

D   Use a fuel filtering system

Question 5

What should you do if you park on the road when it's foggy?

A   Leave dipped headlights and fog lights switched on

B   Leave dipped headlights switched on

C   Leave sidelights switched on

D   Leave main-beam headlights switched on

Question 3

D - Never overtake on the left, unless the traffic is moving in queues and the queue on your right is moving more slowly than the one you're in. Don't be tempted to keep changing lanes to join a faster queue; you'll find they all slow down and speed up at various intervals.

Question 4

A - Fuel spilled on the road is a serious danger to other road users, especially motorcyclists. To prevent this from happening, make sure the filler cap is secure after refuelling.

Question 5

C - If you have to park your vehicle in foggy conditions, try to find a place to park off the road. If this isn't possible, park on the road facing in the same direction as the traffic. Leave your sidelights switched on and make sure they're clean.

Question 6 *

You see these markings on the kerbside. When are you allowed to stop there to unload your vehicle?

A   Not at any time

B   During the working day

C   Outside the working day

D   During the times shown

Question 7

Other drivers may sometimes flash their headlights at you. In which situation are they allowed to do this?

A   To warn of a radar speed trap ahead

B   To show that they are giving way to you

C   To warn you of their presence

D   To let you know there is a fault with your vehicle

Answers

Question 6

A - Loading or unloading is not permitted at any time where double yellow stripes mark the kerb edge. A single yellow stripe would allow loading and unloading during times shown on nearby signs.

Question 7

C - If other drivers flash their headlights, this isn't a signal to show priority. The flashing of headlights has the same meaning as sounding the horn: it's a warning of their presence. Always be very wary in this situation and make sure that you know what the other person intends and that it is safe for whatever you intend to do.

Question 8

Your vehicle is fitted with air-assisted hydraulic brakes. What fault would you suspect if the brake pedal becomes hard to press?

A The brake linings are worn

B The brake system has a loss of vacuum

C The brake shoes need adjusting

D The brake system requires more fluid

Question 9

Trams can move both quietly and quickly. What other feature of trams should you be especially aware of?

A They can't steer to avoid you

B They don't have a horn

C They can't stop for other vehicles

D They don't have lights

Question 10

Your engine catches fire. What should you do before attempting to put the fire out?

A Open the engine housing wide

B Drive to the nearest fire station

C Empty the air tanks

D Shut off the fuel supply

Answers

Question 8

B - A fault in the vacuum pump could be the cause of a stiff brake pedal. There could also be a leaking connection allowing air into the vacuum. Don't continue your journey until the fault has been fixed.

Question 9

A - Electric trams run on rails and can't steer to avoid you. Keep a lookout for trams in areas where they operate, as they move very quietly and you might not hear them approaching.

Question 10

D - An engine fire is serious. If the fire breaches the fuel lines, it can easily spread to the fuel tank. If that happens, both the vehicle and its cargo will probably be lost. Therefore, your priority is to shut off the fuel supply.

Question 11

The law requires the minimum tread depth to be present over what proportion of your lorries tyres?

A   25%

B   50%

C   60%

D   75%

Question 12

You break down on a motorway. You need to call for help. Why may it be better to use an emergency roadside telephone rather than a mobile phone?

A   It connects you to a local garage

B   Using a mobile phone will distract other drivers

C   It allows easy location by the emergency services

D   Mobile phones don't work on motorways

Answers

Question 11

D - You must have the minimum tread depth for your vehicle across at least three quarters (75%) of the surface of each of your tyres.

Question 12

C - On a motorway, it's best to use a roadside emergency telephone so that the emergency services are able to find you easily. The location of the nearest telephone is shown by an arrow on marker posts at the edge of the hard shoulder. If you use a mobile, the operator will need to know your exact location. Before you call, find out the number on the nearest marker post. This number will identify your exact location.

Question 13

What is the purpose of the green area marked on the road in this picture?

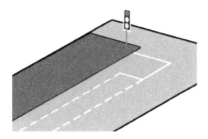

A   To allow room for pedestrians to cross the road

B   To allow space for large vehicles to turn

C   To allow you to overshoot the stop line

D   To allow cyclists to position in front of other traffic

Question 14 *

What does this sign mean?

A   Dual-carriageway ends

B   Merging traffic on both sides

C   There is a fork in the road

D   Road narrows both sides

Question 13

D - Advanced stop lines allow cyclists to take a position ahead of other traffic. When the green signal shows, they then have the time and space to move off in front of the following traffic.

Question 14

D - The road is about to narrow on both sides, you need to be more aware of any overtaking or oncoming traffic.

Question 15 *

Following a long spell of hot dry weather, it's now starting to rain. What do you need to be aware of?

A   There may be an increased risk of skidding

B   The cleaner road surface will give a better grip

C   Braking distances will be shortened

D   The road surface may start to break up

Question 16 *

You're driving a vehicle which is fitted with an analogue tachograph. Which of these should you do?

A   Use no more than one chart per week

B   Change the chart at every stop

C   Keep a separate written diary

D   Be sure to carry enough approved charts

Question 15

A - When it stays dry for some time, deposits such as oil and rubber can build up on the road surface. When rain then falls onto this mixture it can result in a very slippery surface until it's washed away. You should make allowances for this when braking and cornering as the risk of skidding can be much greater.

Question 16

D - You must carry enough charts with you to ensure that they last until the end of your journey. They must also be kept clean and free from damage.

Question 17

What do these signs count down to?

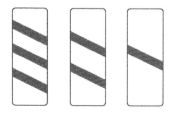

A   A primary road junction

B   A roadside rest area

C   A service station

D   A concealed level crossing

Question 18

What does air suspension help to protect?

A   Underground services

B   The fuel system

C   Tachograph accuracy

D   Engine emissions

Answers

Question 17

D - You will find these were there is a level crossing which is hidden from view. When you see these signs, reduce your speed. You may well have to stop at the level crossing, or there may already be traffic queuing ahead.

Question 18

A - Air suspension reduces the pounding of the vehicle on an uneven road surface. This, in turn, reduces the vibrations transmitted to buildings and underground services along the route.

Question 19

You arrive at an incident. There is no danger from fire or further collisions. What is your first priority when attending to an unconscious motorcyclist?

A   Check whether they are breathing normally

B   Check whether they are bleeding

C   Check whether they have any broken bones

D   Check whether their helmet can be removed

Question 20

In ideal conditions, how much room should you try to leave on your left when passing parked cars?

A   The width of a door mirror

B   About half a metre

C   A minimum of two metres

D   The width of a door

Question 21

You are about to emerge from a junction. Your passenger tells you it is clear. When should you rely on their judgement?

A   Never; you should always look for yourself

B   When the roads are very busy

C   When the roads are very quiet

D   Only when they are a qualified driver

111

Answers

Question 19

A - At the scene of an incident, always be aware of danger from further collisions or fire. The first priority when dealing with an unconscious person is to ensure they're breathing normally. If they're having difficulty breathing, follow the DR ABC code.

Question 20

D - Wherever possible you should leave enough room to avoid a car door should it happen to swing open. On narrow roads or where oncoming traffic prevents this, you should slow down in order to minimise the risk and to give you more time to react.

Question 21

A - Your passenger may be inexperienced in judging traffic situations, may have a poor view or may not have seen a potential hazard. You're responsible for your own safety and that of your passenger. Always make your own checks to be sure it's safe to pull out.

Question 22

The road is wet. Why might a motorcyclist steer round drain covers on a bend?

A   To avoid puncturing the tyres on the edge of the drain covers

B   To help judge the bend using the drain covers as marker points

C   To avoid splashing pedestrians on the pavement

D   To prevent the motorcycle sliding on the metal drain covers

Question 23 *

You are driving a lorry which weighs over 7.5 tonnes. What does this sign mean to you?

A   You can enter this road to pick up your cargo

B   You can enter this road but cannot load your lorry

C   You cannot enter this road at all

D   You must unload your lorry before entering the road

Answers

Question 22

D - Other drivers or riders may have to change course due to the size or characteristics of their vehicle. Understanding this will help you to anticipate their actions. Motorcyclists and cyclists will be checking the road ahead for uneven or slippery surfaces, especially in wet weather. They may need to move across their lane to avoid surface hazards such as potholes and drain covers.

Question 23

A - Vehicles over the weight shown must not enter this road, unless they need access to premises at which they are going to be loading or dropping off cargo.

Question 24

During your working day, you change to another vehicle with the same type of tachograph. How should you keep your tachograph record up-to-date?

A   Use the chart that is already in the other vehicle

B   Record your driving hours in a record book

C   Install a new chart in the other vehicle

D   Take the chart with you and use it in the other vehicle

Question 25

You're following a cyclist. What should you do when you wish to turn left just ahead?

A   Hold back until the cyclist has passed the junction

B   Go around the cyclist at the junction

C   Pull alongside the cyclist and stay level until after the junction

D   Overtake the cyclist before you reach the junction

Question 26 *

Driving rules state that your minimum daily rest is 11 hours. On three days of the week this may be reduced to what minimum length of time?

A   7 hours

B   8 hours

C   9 hours

D   10 hours

Question 24

D - If you change vehicles during the working day, you should take your chart with you and use it in the next vehicle. This isn't always possible, however, as charts produced by different manufacturers may not be interchangeable. In this case, you should use another chart, making sure that all the information for the day is recorded.

Question 25

A - Make allowances for cyclists, and give them plenty of room. The size of your vehicle and the noise it makes can be very intimidating. Be patient and turn behind them after they've passed the junction.

Question 26

C - You must have a minimum daily rest of 11 consecutive hours. A minimum reduced daily rest period is any period of rest of at least 9 hours.

Question 27

On a motorway, what is an emergency refuge area used for?

A When your vehicle has broken down

B If you think you'll be involved in a road rage incident

C For a police patrol to park and watch traffic

D For construction and road workers to store emergency equipment

Question 28 *

You are driving on the left of this road. When may you cross the centre lines?

A You must not cross them at all

B When overtaking another driver

C When passing an obstruction

D When you can see it is clear ahead

Answers

Question 27

A - Emergency refuge areas are built at the side of the hard shoulder. If you break down, try to get your vehicle into the refuge, where there's an emergency telephone. The phone connects directly to a control centre. Remember to take care when rejoining the motorway, especially if the hard shoulder is being used as a running lane.

Question 28

C - With double white lines, if the nearest line to you is solid then you may only cross it in certain circumstances. One of those is if you have to pass a stationary obstruction.

Question 29 *

You see a learner driver starting to pull out of a junction close on your left. What action should you take?

A Reduce speed and be ready to pull back in case they continue

B Carry on as normal as their instructor will stop them

C Slow down and wave them out of the junction

D Move into a wide position so that you can pass them if they pull out

Question 30 *

You are on a busy dual-carriageway; the following driver is much too close to your rear. What can you do to lower the risk?

A Increase the gap between you and the vehicle ahead

B Pick up speed to increase the distance behind

C Slow right down until the other driver overtakes

D Signal left to let the other driver know they can overtake

Question 31

What's the purpose of a catalytic converter?

A To reduce the risk of fire

B To reduce fuel consumption

C To reduce harmful exhaust gases

D To reduce engine wear

Question 29

A - Learner drivers can be unpredictable and may lose control of the car. You should be courteous and maintain a safe distance, allowing for any mistakes that they might make. Never wave other road users on; you may put them into danger from someone else.

Question 30

A - If they wish to overtake at any point, you should leave that decision up to them and maintain a steady speed while gradually opening up space ahead. If you have plenty of space in front, then you will have more time to react if traffic suddenly slows down. This will lessen the risk of the following driver running into you.

Question 31

C - Catalytic converters reduce a large percentage of harmful exhaust emissions. They work more efficiently when the engine has reached its normal working temperature.

Question 32

You are convicted of driving after drinking too much alcohol. How could this affect your insurance?

A   Your insurance may become invalid

B   The amount of excess you pay will be reduced

C   You will only be able to get third-party cover

D   Cover will only be given for driving cars

Question 33

Which sign means 'uneven road'?

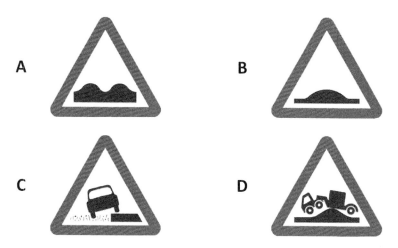

Answers

Question 32

A - Driving while under the influence of drink or drugs can invalidate your insurance. It also endangers yourself and others. The risk isn't worth taking.

Question 33

A - Some signs can look similar to others but each one has a different meaning. For example, this one looks a little like the sign for a hump bridge. Learn the meaning of every sign to prepare yourself for how to react to them.

Question 34

Where would you see this sign?

A   At the end of a dual carriageway

B   At a road narrowing

C   At the end of a one-way street

D   At the beginning of a contra-flow system

Question 35

How should you stand when you're lifting a heavy object?

A   In a stable position

B   Leaning backwards

C   With your legs straight

D   Keeping your feet together

Question 34

B - This sign will be used where the road narrows, often as a result of traffic calming measures. When you see this you should give way to oncoming traffic.

Question 35

A - Always think of your own and others' physical safety before lifting any heavy object. Plan the lift and move any other items out of the way. Decide whether you need assistance.

Question 36

At the scene of a crash, a casualty is in contact with live electrical cables. What should you use to break the electrical connection?

A   A length of wood

B   A metal pole

C   Woollen gloves

D   A damp piece of cloth

Question 37 *

What type of vehicle might you see with a flashing green light on top?

A   An agricultural vehicle

B   A road sweeper

C   An invalid carriage

D   An emergency doctor's car

Question 38

You've broken down on a motorway. In which direction should you walk to find the nearest emergency telephone?

A   With the traffic flow

B   Follow the marker posts

C   Facing oncoming traffic

D   In the direction of the nearest exit

Answers

Question 36

A - At the scene of an incident, if there are any casualties who are in contact with live electricity, don't touch them with your hands — even if you're wearing gloves. You should use a dry, non-conducting item, such as a wooden sweeping brush or plastic spade. You mustn't give first aid until you're sure the electrical contact has been broken, otherwise you'll be putting yourself in danger.

Question 37

D - A doctor is allowed to put a flashing green light on top of their car when they are on an emergency call. If you see one of these you should give way to them if you can do so safely.

Question 38

B - Along the hard shoulder there are marker posts at 100-metre intervals. These will direct you to the nearest emergency telephone

Question 39

Where do most sleep-related vehicle incidents occur?

A   In town centres

B   On motorways

C   On rural roads

D   On tourist routes

Question 40 *

Why do some motorways have variable speed limits?

A   To reduce traffic bunching at peak times

B   To encourage eco-safe driving methods

C   To compensate for poor road surfaces

D   To keep noise down when passing urban areas

Answers

Question 39

B - Driving at a constant speed for long periods, such as on a motorway, can cause drowsiness. Falling asleep while driving accounts for a significant proportion of vehicle incidents. You should plan and take regular rest stops, but if you feel the onset of tiredness between these breaks, stop and rest in a safe place.

Question 40

A - Variable speed limits are used when traffic is busy, and when there are incidents and lane closures. This helps to keep traffic moving at a steady varying speed instead of the normal 'stop start' situation which normally occurs at these times.

Question 41

The road outside this school is marked with yellow zig-zag lines. What do these lines mean?

A   You may wait here when making deliveries

B   You may park here only when loading

C   You mustn't wait or park your vehicle here at all

D   You must stay with your vehicle if you park here

Question 42

What does this sign mean?

A   Side winds

B   Airport ahead

C   Slippery road

D   Flooding

Answers

Question 41

C - The markings are designed to keep the area clear of traffic so that children can cross the road safely without anything blocking their view or hiding them from others.

Question 42

A - You may see this sign in areas where the road is surrounded by open ground. You need to be aware that strong crosswinds could blow you off course.

Question 43 *

What does this road sign mean?

A   No parking on the right

B   No cars are allowed

C   Two-way traffic

D   No overtaking

Question 44

Which of the following types of glasses shouldn't be worn when driving at night?

A   Half-moon

B   Varifocal

C   Bifocal

D   Tinted

Question 43

D - You must not overtake any other motor vehicle when you see this sign by the road.

Question 44

D - If you're driving at night or in poor visibility, tinted lenses will reduce the efficiency of your vision by reducing the amount of light reaching your eyes.

Question 45

What period of time makes up a driver's week?

A   00.00 hours Sunday to 24.00 hours the following Saturday

B   Any 7 consecutive days

C   00.00 hours Monday to 24.00 hours the following Sunday

D   Any 56 hours driven

Question 46 *

Which of the following will have an effect on the stopping distance of your lorry?

A   The traffic ahead of you

B   The condition of your tyres

C   The light conditions

D   The position of following traffic

133

Question 45

C - A driver's week is defined as a period from 00.00 hours on Monday to 24.00 hours the following Sunday.

Question 46

B - There are a number of factors which will affect the distance it takes for you to stop. One of the most important is the condition of your tyres. You should make a regular check to ensure that they are in good condition and have a good amount of tread on them.

Question 47 *

What does this sign mean?

A   No motor vehicles

B   Motor cars and motorcycles only

C   Motorcycles have priority

D   All vehicles prohibited

Question 48 *

What does this warning light on the instrument panel mean?

A   Low oil pressure

B   Battery discharge

C   Braking-system fault

D   A door is open

Question 47

A - The sign prohibits all motor vehicles from proceeding. Cyclists, horse drawn carriages etc. are still allowed to continue.

Question 48

C - If this warning sign lights up on your dashboard you should call for help and get your brake system checked immediately.

Question 49

When may you use your vehicle's hazard warning lights while it is moving?

A   When you have just overtaken another vehicle

B   When one of your lights has failed

C   When you need to reverse for some distance

D   When you are on a motorway and traffic ahead slows suddenly

Question 50 *

You approach a pelican crossing which goes straight across the road with a central island. The amber light is flashing and someone is walking towards you from the other side. What should you do?

A   Stop and allow them to cross

B   Stop only if they are about to step onto your side

C   Drive on if traffic on the other side has started moving

D   Drive on as they are not on your side

Question 49

D - While moving, hazard warning lights may only be used on a motorway or unrestricted dual carriageway to warn drivers behind of a need to slow down, due to a hazard ahead.

Question 50

A - A pelican crossing that goes straight across the road in two parts must be treated as one continuous crossing. The lights controlling the crossing show to traffic approaching from both directions. You must give way to pedestrians who are still crossing when the amber light is flashing even if they are at the other side.

Test Four

Question 1

What can you add to diesel fuel to prevent it from becoming less effective at low temperatures?

A Anti-freeze

B Petrol

C Paraffin

D Anti-waxing additives

Question 2 *

You want to continue ahead at a crossroads where there are no road markings. There are other vehicles approaching from your right and left. Who has priority?

A No-one has priority

B The faster vehicle

C The vehicle from the right

D The vehicle from the left

Question 3

What does it mean when there are double red lines running along the edge of a road?

A Limited loading

B Bus route

C Short-term parking

D No stopping

141

Answers

Question 1

D - In extremely cold weather, you should use diesel fuel with anti-waxing additives to stop the fuel lines from freezing up. During the winter months, these additives are usually put in by the fuel companies.

Question 2

A - No-one has priority in this situation. Unmarked crossroads should be approached with plenty of caution. Slow down, take good observation in all directions before you emerge or make a turn. Proceed only when you're sure it's safe to do so.

Question 3

D - Double red lines indicate that you're on a Red Route and in a no-stopping area. Red Routes also have single red lines, with signs showing the times that restrictions are in force. There are also parking and loading boxes, which have signs explaining the restrictions that apply.

Question 4

You want to turn right at a roundabout marked with two right-turn lanes. What should you do if there's ample room for your vehicle in either lane?

A   Use the right-hand of the two lanes

B   Use the left-hand lane, then move to the right as you enter the roundabout

C   Use the left-hand of the two lanes

D   Use the right-hand lane, then move to the left as you enter the roundabout

Question 5

You are driving through a tunnel. What should you do if your vehicle breaks down?

A   Remain in your vehicle

B   Switch on hazard warning lights

C   Wait for the police to find you

D   Rely on CCTV cameras seeing you

Question 6 *

Front fog lights may be used when visibility is down to what distance?

A   100 metres

B   150 metres

C   200 metres

D   250 metres

Answers

Question 4

C - Using the left-hand lane will make it easier for you to leave the roundabout. If you use the right-hand lane, there could be traffic on your left and in your blind spot when you reach your exit and try to move back to the left.

Question 5

B - If your vehicle breaks down in a tunnel, it could present a danger to other traffic. First, switch on your hazard warning lights. If there are passengers in your vehicle, take them to the nearest exit point. You should then call for help from an emergency telephone. Don't rely on being found by the police or being seen by a CCTV camera. The longer a vehicle stays in an exposed position, the more danger it poses to other traffic.

Question 6

A - Your fog lights must only be used when visibility is reduced to 100 metres (328 feet) or less. You need to be familiar with the layout of your dashboard so you're aware if your fog lights have been switched on in error, or you've forgotten to switch them off.

Question 7

After the registration of a new lorry weighing over 3500 kilos, when will it need its first MOT?

A   After 1 year

B   After 2 years

C   After 3 years

D   After 4 years

Question 8

What is the national speed limit on a motorway for a lorry weighing over 7.5 tonnes?

A   50 mph (80 km/h)

B   55 mph (88 km/h)

C   60 mph (96 km/h)

D   70 mph (112 km/h)

Question 9

When should you check your vehicle's spray-suppression equipment?

A   Only when you will be using a motorway

B   Before setting out on every journey

C   Only at the start of winter as a pre-winter check

D   Once per year before the MOT test

Question 7

A - Lorries over 3500 kilos must be presented for an MOT 12 months after first being registered, and again every year after that.

Question 8

C - Be aware of, and obey, all speed limits. On a motorway, any lorry that's articulated, towing a trailer, or over 7.5 tonnes mustn't exceed 60 mph (96 km/h).

Question 9

A - You should always check all your spray-suppression equipment before a journey. Don't ignore it just because it's dry when you set out. The weather can change on the way.

What does this sign mean?

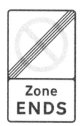

A   End of cycle route

B   End of clearway

C   End of restricted speed area

D   End of restricted parking area

Question 11

You are driving an empty curtain-sided vehicle. Why might you consider tying the curtains open?

A   To reduce the effect of side wind

B   To use less fuel

C   It is a legal requirement

D   To prevent the curtains from tearing

Question 10

D - Even though you've left the restricted area, make sure that you park where you won't endanger other road users or cause an obstruction.

Question 11

A - Closed curtains on large empty vehicles can hold the wind. Strong side wind can blow a semi-trailer off course and, in severe cases, can blow the whole vehicle over onto its side. To reduce the risk of this happening, you should tie the curtains open.

Question 12

Which road users are most at danger from the turbulence from your vehicle?

A   Tractor drivers

B   Lorry drivers

C   Car drivers towing caravans

D   Coach drivers

Question 13

Where must the repair of a speed limiter be carried out?

A   At any DVSA site

B   At any dealer centre

C   At the depot by a mechanic

D   At an authorised centre

Question 14

What does a sign with a brown background show?

A   Primary roads

B   Minor roads

C   Tourist directions

D   Motorway route

Question 12

C - Remember that the buffeting caused by large vehicles can affect other road users, including

- cars towing caravans
- motorcyclists
- cyclists
- horse riders.

Question 13

D - Speed limiters may only be repaired by authorised speed-limiter centres. They'll ensure that all the connections are sealed and that the system is tamperproof.

Question 14

C - Signs with a brown background give directions to places of interest. They're often seen on a motorway, directing you along the easiest route to the attraction.

Question 15

You're new to using tachographs, what could happen if you break the regulations?

A   You could receive a heavy fine

B   You could have your driving licence revoked

C   You could receive the first of three warnings

D   You could be sent on a training course

Question 16

What must you do before you start reversing?

A   Look all around

B   Remove your seat belt

C   Use an audible warning device

D   Change the tachograph mode

Question 17 *

You have a hand held mobile phone in your vehicle. What should you do to make a call whilst in traffic?

A   Dial the number and then put the handset back into a cradle

B   Find a safe place to stop before you pick the phone up

C   Wait until you're stationary at traffic lights

D   Pull up on double yellow lines with your hazard lights on

Question 15

A - The driver must take responsibility and follow the drivers' hours and tachograph rules. Failure to do so can result in legal action and penalties such as a fine.

Question 16

A - Large or long vehicles have many blind spots. It's vital to check all these areas before starting to reverse and then make sure you keep checking all around while completing the manoeuvre. Get someone to help you if you can.

Question 17

B - It is unsafe and against the law to use a hand held phone while driving, even when stationary in traffic queues. You MUST find a safe place to pull over and stop before using it and that does not include double yellow lines which indicate that waiting restrictions apply.

Question 18 *

It is a bright and sunny day. You are about to drive through a tunnel. What should you do before you enter it?

A   Turn off the radio

B   Take of your sunglasses

C   Switch off your mobile phone

D   Turn on the demisters

Question 19

When would you use 'kickdown' on a vehicle that has automatic transmission?

A   To apply the emergency brakes

B   To give quicker acceleration

C   To stop more smoothly

D   To go down a steep hill

Question 20

Why do energy-saving tyres contribute to better fuel economy?

A   They're much easier to manufacture

B   They have a reduced rolling resistance

C   They allow you to travel at higher speeds

D   They allow heat to disperse more quickly

Question 18

B - Tunnels can be quite dark; you need to be able to see properly so if you are wearing sunglasses they should be removed until you reach the end.

Question 19

B - Depending on road speed, pressing the accelerator pedal firmly to the floor will activate a switch that allows the gearbox to select a lower gear for improved acceleration.

Question 20

B - Less fuel will be used to move your vehicle at the same speed if you use a tyre with reduced rolling resistance, rather than one of normal construction. Low-rolling-resistance tyres aren't all the same; they have ratings for rolling resistance, wet-weather grip and noise. Specialists can advise on the best tyres for specific requirements.

Question 21

Your lorry has a maximum authorised mass of more than 7.5 tonnes. What does this sign mean to you?

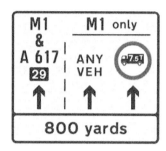

A   You can only use the right-hand lane

B   You must not use the right-hand lane

C   You can use the middle or right-hand lane

D   You can't leave the motorway at this junction

Question 22

There are no speed-limit signs on the road. How is a 30 mph limit indicated?

A   By double or single yellow lines

B   By hazard warning lines

C   By pedestrian islands

D   By street lighting

Question 21

B - At motorway roadworks, some lanes may be narrower than normal and large vehicles may not be allowed to use those lanes. Look for weight-limit signs to check for any lanes that you can't use. Move to the appropriate lane in good time.

Question 22

D - There's a 30 mph speed limit where there are street lights unless signs show another limit.

Question 23

What do these road markings mean?

A Keep two chevrons apart

B One way street

C Do not cross

D Speed humps

Question 24

Which of these vehicles will be most at risk of 'roll-over' when laden?

A

B

C

D

Question 23

C - These markings are seen on a motorway separating lanes, normally where a slip road joins the motorway or where motorways separate. You MUST not cross these where the border is solid except in an unavoidable emergency.

Question 24

A - 'Roll-over' usually happens as a result of the inside rear wheels of an articulated vehicle starting to lift when the driver changes direction sharply. This tends to happen when a driver is changing direction to leave a roundabout. If the load moves during the change of direction, the vehicle is increasingly at risk of rolling over. The problem often involves vehicles carrying fluids in bulk.

Question 25

Where should you not use a breakdown warning triangle?

A On a dual carriageway

B On a single-track road

C On a narrow country road

D On a motorway

Question 26

What does this sign mean?

A Queues likely

B Car lane only

C Single file traffic

D Keep your distance

Answers

Question 25

D - If your vehicle breaks down, be aware of the danger to, and from, other traffic. Get your vehicle off the road if possible. Use a warning triangle to alert other road users to the obstruction but NOT when you're on a motorway. The risk of walking along the hard shoulder to place the triangle is too great.

Question 26

A - When you see this sign, beware of traffic queues ahead. Check your mirrors and reduce your speed.

Be patient when you're delayed by traffic queues and reduce the possibility of being involved in an incident. Research shows that you make poor decisions when you're angry, so you're less likely to spot and respond safely to hazards.

Question 27

What is the final thing you should do after re-coupling a trailer?

A   Connect the brake lines

B   Release the trailer parking brake

C   Connect the electrical lines

D   Raise the trailer legs

Question 28

When must you notify telephone companies that you are moving a high load?

A   When the load height exceeds 4.00 metres [13 feet]

B   When the load height exceeds 4.30 metres [14 feet 2 inches]

C   When the load height exceeds 5.00 metres [16 feet 6 inches]

D   When the load height exceeds 5.25 metres [17 feet 6 inches]

Question 29

Before starting driving, which of the following should you complete on the centre field of your tachograph chart?

A   The amount of daily rest taken prior to starting the shift

B   The name and address of your employer

C   The starting point of your day's journey

D   Details of the goods carried

Answers

Question 27

B - It's important to work methodically when uncoupling or recoupling a tractor unit and trailer. After recoupling, check that all connections, systems and lights are working correctly before finally releasing the trailer parking brake.

Question 28

D - You should tell telephone companies about your intended route when planning the movement of loads over 5.25 metres (17 feet 6 inches) high. You should tell them in plenty of time before making the journey.

Question 29

C - Before starting your journey, you must record a number of items on your tachograph chart. One of these is where the journey begins.

Question 30

You're stopped by a police officer for a suspected motoring offence. Which document will you always be asked to produce?

A Your driving licence

B The vehicle tachograph

C Vehicle registration document

D Vehicle service record

Question 31

Bus and lorry tyres have codes on their side walls. What do these codes refer to?

A Speed capability

B Running pressure

C Tread depth

D Minimum temperature

Question 32

Your vehicle catches fire while driving through a tunnel. It is still driveable. What should you do?

A Drive it out of the tunnel if you can do so

B Leave it where it is, with the engine running

C Stop, and wait for help to arrive

D Pull up, then walk to an emergency telephone

Question 30

A - You must stop if you've been involved in a collision which results in injury or damage. The police may ask to see your driving licence and insurance details at the time or later at a police station.

Question 31

A - Codes shown on the tyre wall refer to the maximum load and speed capability of the tyre.

Question 32

A - If it's possible, and you can do so without causing further danger, it may be safer to drive a vehicle that's on fire out of a tunnel. The greatest danger in a tunnel fire is smoke and suffocation.

Question 33

What is the principal braking system on a lorry called?

A   The endurance brake

B   The jake brake

C   The service brake

D   The exhaust brake

Question 34

When is a high-sided vehicle most affected by side wind?

A   When it is travelling empty

B   When it is being reversed

C   When it is stationary

D   When it is travelling loaded

Answers

Question 33

C - The service brake is usually operated by the brake pedal. It's used to control the speed of the vehicle and to bring it to a halt safely. It may also incorporate an anti-lock braking system.

Question 34

A - Take care if you're driving an empty high-sided vehicle when it's windy. Watch for places where the conditions could suddenly change, such as a gap between buildings or when passing under a bridge. Reduce your speed and stay alert for other road users who are also affected by these weather conditions.

Question 35 *

What does this sign mean?

A   No entry for vehicles over 32.6 tonnes

B   Warning of lorries crossing ahead

C   No vehicles over length shown

D   Distance to lorry parking area

Question 36

You have parked on the roadside. What must you do before leaving the vehicle?

A   Remove your personal items

B   Switch off the tachograph

C   Stop the engine

D   Reset the retarder

Question 35

C - You need to know the length of your vehicle as well as its weight, height and width. Places where the length of your vehicle may be relevant are

• road tunnels
• level crossings
• ferries
• bridges

Question 36

C - Before leaving your vehicle parked, you must stop the engine. The parking brake must be set and the vehicle should be safe and secure when you leave the cab.

Question 37

What does this sign mean?

A   No entry for traffic turning left

B   No through road on the left

C   Turn left for ferry terminal

D   Turn left for parking area

Question 38

What does this tachograph symbol mean?

A   Driver at rest

B   Chart not required

C   Other work

D   Driving time

Question 37

B - This sign shows you that you can't get through to another route by turning left at the junction ahead.

Question 38

D - Each activity has a different symbol. You should know what they mean, so that you can select the correct one. You're responsible for recording all your activities correctly.

Question 39

Which of these is a hazard warning line?

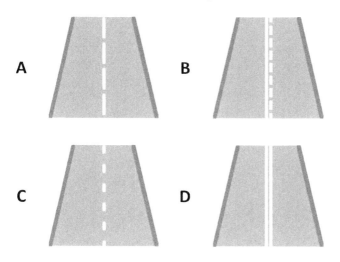

A

B

C

D

Question 40

You're driving an articulated lorry on a narrow road. There's a left-hand bend ahead. Why may you need to move out before driving around the bend?

A   To leave more room for braking

B   To make sure oncoming drivers see you

C   To prevent anyone from overtaking

D   To make room for the trailer cutting in

Question 39

A - You need to know the difference between various types of road marking. If there's a hazard ahead, the single centre lines are longer and the gaps shorter. This gives you advance warning of an unspecified hazard.

Question 40

D - You should always be aware of the amount of room your trailer needs when it's going around bends and corners. If you need to go onto the other side of the road, make sure there's no oncoming traffic before you move out.

Question 41 *

You're approaching a set of traffic lights. They have been on green for quite a while. What should you do?

A   Pick up speed before they change

B   Check your mirrors and prepare to stop

C   Change into a lower gear

D   Maintain a steady speed

Question 42

You are driving an articulated lorry that has three air lines connected to the trailer. What is the purpose of the red line?

A   It is the emergency line

B   It is the service line

C   It is the auxiliary line

D   It is the electrical line

Question 43

You are often involved in the carrying of high-value goods. What security measures can you adopt

A   Keep your journeys to a strict routine

B   Give lifts to people for added security

C   Vary your routes and rest stops

D   Tell plenty of people about your journey

Answers

Question 41

B - Lights which have green for a long time are possibly about to change. You should check your mirrors, ease off the gas and be ready to stop in case they do. Particularly if you are driving a loaded vehicle; braking late could cause problems and you need to show good planning on the approach to any potential hazard.

Question 42

A - The red emergency line is common to both two-line and three-line brake systems. The other colours are :

- blue – auxiliary
- yellow – service

Question 43

C - When carrying high-value goods, you can become a target for thieves. Avoid developing a set routine or pattern. Vary your routes whenever possible to make it difficult for thieves to predict when and where your cargo can be intercepted.

Question 44

You've broken down on a two-way road. You have a warning triangle. At least how far from your vehicle should you place the warning triangle?

A 5 metres (16 feet)

B 25 metres (82 feet)

C 45 metres (147 feet)

D 100 metres (328 feet)

Question 45

Why should you switch off your rear fog lights when the fog has cleared?

A To allow your headlights to work better

B To prevent dazzling following drivers

C To help prevent battery drain

D To stop the engine losing power

Question 44

C - Advance warning triangles fold flat and don't take up much room. Use one to warn other road users if your vehicle has broken down or if there has been an incident. Place it at least 45 metres (147 feet) behind your vehicle (or the incident), on the same side of the road or verge. Place it further back if the scene is hidden by, for example, a bend, hill or dip in the road. Don't use warning triangles on motorways.

Question 45

B - Don't forget to switch off your fog lights when the weather improves. You could be prosecuted for driving with them on in good visibility. The high intensity of rear fog lights can dazzle following drivers and make your brake lights difficult to notice.

Question 46

Who's responsible for making sure that a vehicle isn't overloaded?

A   The driver of the vehicle

B   The licensing authority

C   The owner of the items being carried

D   The person who loaded the vehicle

Question 47

You're driving down a long, steep hill. You suddenly notice that your brakes aren't working as well as normal. What's the usual cause of this?

A   Air in the brake fluid

B   Badly adjusted brakes

C   Oil on the brakes

D   The brakes overheating

Question 46

A - Carrying heavy loads will affect control and the vehicle's handling characteristics. If the vehicle you're driving is overloaded, you'll be held responsible.

Question 47

D - Continuous use of the brakes can cause them to start overheating. This is more likely to happen on vehicles fitted with drum brakes, but it can apply to disc brakes as well. Using a lower gear will assist the braking and help you to keep control of your vehicle.

Why are these yellow lines painted across the road?

A To help you choose the correct lane

B To help you keep the correct separation distance

C To make you aware of your speed

D To tell you the distance to the roundabout

What must you do when you park a lorry weighing more than 7.5 tonnes on a verge for essential loading?

A Sign the collection note

B Display an orange badge

C Obtain the owner's permission

D Make sure the lorry is always attended

Answers

Question 48

C - These lines are often found on the approach to a roundabout or a dangerous junction. They give you extra warning to adjust your speed. Look well ahead and do this in good time.

Question 49

D - Goods vehicles with a maximum authorised mass of more than 7.5 tonnes (including any trailer) mustn't be parked on a verge without police permission. The only exception is when this is essential for loading and unloading. In these cases, the vehicle mustn't be left unattended.

You see this sign on a motorway, what is it telling you?

A   You should move to the lane on your left

B   You must not move into the left hand lane

C   You must leave the motorway at the next exit

D   You should move across to the hard shoulder

Question 50

A - Overhead signs on motorways will give instructions such as temporary speed limits and lane closures. This sign tells you to move into the next lane on your left.

Test Five

Question 1

The Driver and Vehicle Standards Agency (DVSA) and the police carry out spot checks for faulty vehicles. What will happen to the vehicle if serious defects are found?

A   It will be impounded until a new driver is found

B   It will be ordered back to the depot to unload goods or passengers

C   It will be restricted to 30 mph for the remainder of the journey

D   It will be prohibited from further use until the defects are rectified

Question 2

You're part-loading a lorry with an empty ISO container. Where should you position it on the trailer?

A   Close to the fifth wheel

B   Over the front axle

C   Close to the trailer edge

D   Over the rear axles

Question 3

Who's responsible for issuing tachograph charts to a bus or lorry driver?

A   The Driver and Vehicle Standards Agency

B   The driver's employer

C   The authorised calibration centre

D   The local MOT testing centre

185

Answers

Question 1

D - DVSA or the police can order an immediate prohibition. The vehicle may be immobilised and you won't be able to drive it until the faults have been rectified. Details are notified to the traffic commissioner. Never use a vehicle that you know is faulty.

Question 2

D - To increase stability and reduce the risk of the trailer wheels lifting when turning, it's preferable to locate part-loads over the rear axle(s).

Question 3

B - The driver's employer is responsible for the issue of tachograph charts. The driver must ensure that the correct information is recorded on the chart.

Question 4

You're driving downhill. How will this affect your vehicle?

A   It will need more engine power

B   It will take longer to stop

C   It will increase fuel consumption

D   It will be easier to change direction

Question 5

You're turning right onto a dual carriageway from a side road. What should you do if your vehicle is too long for the gap in the central reservation?

A   Wait until it is clear in both directions

B   When it's safe, move to the centre of the road and wait

C   Move out, blocking traffic from the right

D   Edge out slowly so other traffic will see you

Question 4

B - When driving downhill, gravity will cause the vehicle to increase speed. More braking effort will be required, and stopping distances will increase. You should make allowances for this by controlling your speed and keeping your distance from other vehicles.

Question 5

A - When your vehicle is too big to fit into the central reservation, you should treat a dual carriageway as one road and wait until the road is clear in both directions before emerging to turn right. If you try to treat it as two separate roads and wait in the middle, your vehicle will overhang the central reservation and could cause a collision.

Question 6

What does this motorway sign mean?

A   You're approaching a long downhill slope

B   You're approaching a long uphill slope

C   You're approaching a 'lorries only' lane

D   You're approaching a service area

Question 7

You're driving a large vehicle on a narrow road with passing places. What will you need to be most aware of?

A   Its length

B   Its roof height

C   Its ground clearance

D   Its weight

189

Answers

Question 6

B - The term 'crawler lane' doesn't mean the lane is only for extremely slow vehicles. It's advising you of an extra lane on the left. Crawler lanes are usually built on sections of road where the length of the gradient is such that some large vehicles will be slowed to the point where they become a hazard for other road users.

Question 7

A - If your vehicle is too long to fit into a passing place, you may need to wait opposite one. This will allow a following or approaching driver to pass. When you use this type of road, you need to plan and look well ahead to avoid meeting another road user at an inappropriate place.

Question 8

You're in the left-hand lane on a three-lane motorway. Why should you check for any vehicles in the right-hand lane before you overtake?

A   They may be moving faster than you

B   They may cut in sharply behind you

C   They may accelerate briskly in front of you

D   They may move back to the middle lane as you move out

Question 9

You're at a road junction, turning into a minor road. What should you do if there are pedestrians crossing the minor road?

A   Stop and wave the pedestrians across

B   Sound your horn to let the pedestrians know that you're there

C   Give way to the pedestrians who are already crossing

D   Carry on; the pedestrians should give way to you

Question 10 *

Why is it a good idea to switch to a local radio station before entering a tunnel?

A   Because the local radio content will be better

B   Because national radio signals will be lost

C   Because it will be compatible with your sat nav

D   Because it may give you information about any problems ahead

Answers

Question 8

D - Vehicles overtaking in the right-hand lane may return to the centre lane when they've finished their manoeuvre. You should look for this before starting to pull out.

Question 9

C - Always look into the road you're entering. If pedestrians are already crossing, be considerate and give way to them. Don't wave or signal them to hurry; they have priority here.

Question 10

D - On the approach to many tunnels, a board will indicate a local channel or radio frequency that you should tune into. This should give a warning of any incident or congestion in the tunnel ahead. Severe loss of life has occurred in tunnel fires. Getting advance warning of any problems ahead will help you to take appropriate action in good time.

Question 11

An enforcement officer keeps one of your tachograph charts. Who should sign the back of the replacement chart?

A   You, the driver

B   Your transport manager

C   The officer

D   The vehicle owner

Question 12

Under EU rules, what's the normal weekly rest period that must be taken?

A   40 hours

B   41 hours

C   42 hours

D   45 hours

Question 13

You're at the scene of an incident. What does it mean if there's a plain orange rectangle displayed on one of the vehicles?

A   It's carrying perishable food

B   It's carrying medical supplies

C   It's carrying dangerous goods

D   It's not laden with goods

Question 11

C - When an enforcement officer keeps a record chart, the driver should ask the officer to sign the back of the replacement chart. They'll need to give their name, telephone number and the number of charts they've kept. The replacement chart must be used to continue the journey. You should always carry more blank charts than you think you'll need.

Question 12

D - The working week is defined as from 00.00 hours on Monday to 24.00 hours on the following Sunday. When taking the weekly rest period, a daily rest period must normally be extended to at least 45 consecutive hours.

Question 13

C - Vehicles that carry dangerous goods have badges displayed on the side and rear. The badges are orange and show the type of material that's being carried. Make a note of this and report it to the emergency services when you contact them.

Question 14

Your vehicle has a maximum authorised mass of 40 tonnes. The tare weight is 10 tonnes. What's your maximum payload?

A   20 tonnes

B   30 tonnes

C   40 tonnes

D   50 tonnes

Question 15

You're driving along a motorway. What should you do if the air-pressure warning device starts to operate?

A   Stop immediately in the lane you're in

B   Continue slowly to the next service area

C   Leave the motorway at the next exit

D   Stop on the hard shoulder as soon as possible

Question 16

You have too much oil in your engine. What could this cause?

A   Oil leaks

B   Low oil pressure

C   Engine overheating

D   Carburettor damage

Answers

Question 14

B - To work out your vehicle's payload, use the following formula: maximum authorised mass (MAM), minus tare weight, equals payload. This is the maximum weight your vehicle can carry.

Question 15

D - If the air-pressure warning activates, you should have enough air to allow you to stop safely on the hard shoulder. Don't delay stopping, as further loss of air may cause the brakes to lock on. Switch on the hazard warning lights. Use the nearest emergency telephone to call for assistance.

Question 16

A - Too much oil in the engine will create excess pressure and could damage engine seals and cause oil leaks. Any excess oil should be drained off.

Question 17

You discover that one of your rear brake-light bulbs has failed. How soon should it be replaced?

A   On return to your base

B   Within 24 hours

C   At the end of your journey

D   Immediately

Question 18 *

What is the best way to drive your vehicle through a ford?

A   Drive through slowly in low gear

B   Drive through quickly in low gear

C   Drive through slowly in high gear

D   Drive through quickly in high gear

Question 17

D - Bulbs should be replaced as soon as you're aware that they've failed. Carry a stock of all the various bulbs used on your vehicle, so you can repair a fault without delay.

Question 18

A - In normal conditions, a ford can be crossed quite safely by driving through it slowly. You need to prevent water from entering through the exhaust by keeping the 'revs' high in a low gear. This can be helped by slipping the clutch if necessary to keep revs high but speed low.

Question 19 *

You're travelling at 60 mph in the left-hand lane of a three-lane motorway. What should you do when there are vehicles about to join from the slip road?

A   Speed up to get past them

B   Maintain a steady speed

C   Quickly brake to give way to them

D   Move to another lane if you can

Question 20 *

A cycle lane is marked by a solid white line. What does this mean?

A   Drivers can use it only when parking

B   Drivers must not use that lane at any time

C   Drivers may use the lane at any time

D   Drivers may only use the lane at certain times

Question 21

You're driving at night with your headlights on full beam. A vehicle is overtaking you. When should you dip your lights?

A   Shortly after the vehicle has passed you

B   You should dip them immediately

C   Only if the other driver dips their headlights

D   As soon as the vehicle is about to pass you

Question 19

D - Plan well ahead when approaching a slip road. If you see traffic joining the motorway, move to another lane if it's safe to do so. This can help the flow of traffic joining the motorway, especially at peak times. You must be careful however not to change lanes unsafely and cause problems for other drivers behind you.

Question 20

B - Cycle lanes which are marked with a continuous solid white line are for cyclists only. You must not drive along it any time. Nor should you park within this area.

Question 21

D - Leaving them on full beam for a few moments as they are pulling out will light the way ahead, but dip your lights as soon as the driver is about to pass you.

Question 22

There's been a collision. A driver is suffering from shock. What should you do?

A   Give them a drink

B   Ask who caused the incident

C   Leave them alone to recover

D   Try to reassure them

Question 23 *

Why should you check your nearside mirror after passing parked cars?

A   To see if they move off after you have passed

B   To check for pedestrians crossing the road

C   To make sure you don't move to the left too soon

D   To make sure that the mirror hasn't been clipped

Question 24

What should you do when you're overtaking at night?

A   Wait until a bend so that you can see oncoming headlights

B   Flash your lights before moving out

C   Put your headlights on full beam

D   Beware of bends in the road ahead

Answers

Question 22

D - A casualty suffering from shock may have injuries that aren't immediately obvious. Call the emergency services, then stay with the person in shock, offering reassurance until the experts arrive.

Question 23

C - As you pass parked cars you should use your nearside mirror and check that you've passed them safely. You need to allow a good safety margin before you move back to the left, particularly if you are driving a long vehicle.

Question 24

D - Don't overtake if there's a possibility of a road junction, bend or brow of a bridge or hill ahead. There are many hazards that are difficult to see in the dark. Only overtake if you're certain that the road ahead is clear. Don't take a chance.

Question 25

What would be affected by a vehicle with faulty suspension?

A Road surfaces

B Acceleration rate

C Tyre pressures

D Engine performance

Question 26

You're making a journey with a co-driver. When the other person is driving, how should you show this time?

A As a daily rest period

B As a weekly rest period

C As a break in daily driving

D As driving time

Question 27

What should you check when you're leaving a motorway after travelling at speed for some time?

A The speedometer

B The fuel level

C The engine temperature

D The brakes

Answers

Question 25

A - If your suspension is damaged, all the weight of the vehicle compresses the road and anything located below it. The vibrations travel through the ground and can also damage surrounding buildings.

Question 26

C - You may only record a break when you're not doing any other type of work. You're allowed to take a break on a double-manned vehicle while the other crew member is driving, but any break must be a minimum of 15 minutes.

Question 27

A - After leaving a motorway or when using a link road between motorways, your speed may be higher than you realise: 50 mph may feel like 30 mph. Check the speedometer and adjust your speed accordingly.

Question 28

While driving at night, you see a pedestrian ahead. What does it mean if they're wearing reflective clothing and carrying a red light?

A   You're approaching men at work

B   You're approaching an incident blackspot

C   You're approaching slow-moving vehicles

D   You're approaching an organised walk

Question 29

You've stopped on a firm, level surface. What's the first thing you must do before you uncouple the trailer?

A   Apply the parking brake

B   Lower the trailer legs to the ground

C   Release the brake air lines

D   Uncouple the electrical lines

Question 30 *

Where are motorcyclists and cyclists particularly vulnerable?

A   At junctions

B   On dual carriageways

C   On country roads

D   In urban areas

Question 28

D - Pedestrians who are part of an organised walk using the road at night should wear bright or reflective clothing. The walker in front should display a white light, while the one at the back should display a red light. Be particularly careful, slow down and give the walkers plenty of room.

Question 29

A - Before leaving the cab, it's very important to secure the vehicle by applying the parking brake. After leaving the cab, apply the trailer parking brake.

Question 30

A - Motorcyclists and cyclists who may be nearer to the kerb than other vehicles can be harder to see when you're emerging from a junction. Their relatively smaller size means that they can also be hidden from view by obstructions such as parked cars and 'street furniture'.

Question 31

What's the maximum fine for driving without insurance?

A   £500

B   £1000

C   £5000

D   Unlimited

Question 32

What should you do if the brake air-pressure warning light comes on while you're driving?

A   Report the fault when you return to your depot

B   Stop and get help without delay

C   Build up the pressure by accelerating

D   Drain the air tanks and continue normally

Question 33

What does it mean if the signs at a bus lane show no times of operation?

A   The lane isn't in operation

B   The lane is only in operation at peak times

C   The lane is only in operation in daylight hours

D   The lane is in operation 24 hours a day

Answers

Question 31

D - It's a serious offence to drive without insurance. As well as an unlimited fine, you may be disqualified or given penalty points.

Question 32

B - When a warning light or device indicating a loss of pressure comes on, you must stop safely and get the fault put right immediately. The safety of you, your load, your passengers and all other road users is at risk.

Question 33

D - Bus -lane signs show the vehicles allowed to use the lane and also its times of operation. Where no times are shown, the bus lane is in operation 24 hours a day.

Question 34

When may vehicles over 7.5 tonnes maximum authorised mass (MAM) use the right-hand lane of a motorway to overtake?

A   When the motorway has three lanes

B   When the motorway has two lanes

C   When vehicles are stopped on the hard shoulder

D   When other vehicles are turning off the motorway

Question 35

Which drivers are given instructions by diamond-shaped signs?

A   Drivers of lorries

B   Drivers of buses

C   Drivers of trams

D   Drivers of tractors

Question 36

Daytime visibility is poor and misty but not seriously reduced. Which lights should you switch on?

A   Headlights and fog lights

B   Front fog lights

C   Dipped headlights

D   Rear fog lights

Question 34

B - Goods and passenger vehicles with a MAM of more than 7.5 tonnes, those required to be fitted with a speed limiter, and vehicles towing trailers must not use the right-hand lane on a motorway with more than two lanes, unless there are exceptional circumstances.

Question 35

C - You need to show caution when driving in areas where trams operate. You might not hear their approach and they can't change direction to avoid you. There may also be crossing points where you'll need to give way to them, or areas specifically reserved for trams, which you aren't allowed to enter.

Question 36

C - Only use your fog lights when visibility is seriously reduced. Use dipped headlights in poor conditions because this helps other road users to see you without the risk of causing dazzle.

Question 37

Where would you see a contraflow bus and cycle lane?

A   On a dual carriageway

B   On a roundabout

C   On an urban motorway

D   On a one-way street

Question 38

What does this sign mean?

A   Danger ahead

B   Tunnel ahead

C   Slippery road

D   Flood water

Question 37

D - The traffic permitted to use a contraflow lane travels in the opposite direction to traffic in the other lanes on the road. They are normally used by bus drivers and cyclists.

Question 38

A - This sign is shown when there is some kind of danger ahead. It may be shown on its own as a general warning for caution; or it may be shown with an information plate below describing the nature of the hazard.

Question 39

When may you stop on an urban clearway?

A   To use a mobile telephone

B   To set down and pick up passengers

C   To ask for directions

D   To load or unload goods

Question 40

At the end of your working week, you've driven a total of 56 hours. Under EU rules, what's the maximum number of hours you can drive in the following week?

A   34

B   36

C   38

D   40

Question 41

A loud buzzer sounds in your vehicle. What's this most likely to indicate?

A   Low oil pressure

B   Low tyre pressure

C   Low air pressure

D   Low fuel level

Question 39

B - Urban clearways have their times of operation clearly signed. You may stop only for as long as is reasonable to pick up or set down passengers. You should ensure that you're not causing an obstruction for other traffic.

Question 40

A - If you've driven a total of 56 hours in any one week, you can only drive for 34 hours in the following week. Keep your own record to make sure that you don't exceed these hours.

Question 41

C - Warning buzzers are linked to many systems on modern vehicles, including the air brakes. A warning light on the dashboard may help you identify the system that's caused the problem. Stop in a safe place until the fault has been identified and put right. Get professional help if necessary.

Question 42 *

What do double yellow lines along the edge of the road mean?

A   No loading at certain times

B   No waiting along this road

C   No stopping at any time

D   No parking without hazard lights

Question 43

Traffic officers operate on motorways and some primary routes in England. What are they authorised to do?

A   Stop and arrest drivers who break the law

B   Repair broken-down vehicles on the motorway

C   Stop and direct anyone on a motorway

D   Issue fixed penalty notices

Question 42

B - Double yellow lines indicate that waiting is not allowed at any time. You can however stop as long as needed to drop off or pick up a load or passengers unless signs show otherwise.

Question 43

C - Traffic officers don't have enforcement powers but are able to stop and direct people on motorways and some 'A' class roads. They only operate in England and work in partnership with the police at incidents, providing a highly trained and visible service. They're recognised by an orange-and-yellow jacket and their vehicle has yellow-and-black markings.

Question 44

What does this sign mean?

A   Minimum speed 30 mph

B   End of minimum speed

C   End of maximum speed

D   Maximum speed 30 mph

Question 45

You're driving a long vehicle. What should you be especially careful of before turning left onto a main road?

A   Cyclists on your left

B   Pedestrians on the opposite kerb

C   Solid white lines in the centre of the road

D   Vehicles directly behind you

Question 44

B - The red slash through the sign indicates that the restriction has ended. In this case, the restriction was a minimum speed limit of 30 mph.

Question 45

A - You should always check your nearside mirror before any change of direction. Be alert for cyclists and motorcyclists who don't realise the potential danger involved in trying to squeeze through on your nearside when you're waiting at a junction.

An injured person has been placed in the recovery position. They're unconscious but breathing normally. What else should be done?

A   Check their airway remains open

B   Press firmly between their shoulders

C   Place their arms by their side

D   Turn them over every few minutes

Question 47

Your vehicle is fully loaded. Where should you be braking when dealing with bends?

A   As close to the bend as possible

B   As you start to turn the wheel

C   When halfway around the bend

D   When driving in a straight line

Question 48

You've been stopped at a roadside check. What would staff from the environmental health department be checking?

A   Licence entitlement

B   Exhaust emissions

C   Tachograph changes

D   Illegal immigrants

Question 46

A - After a casualty has been placed in the recovery position, make sure their airway remains open and monitor their condition until medical help arrives. Where possible, don't move a casualty unless there's further danger.

Question 47

D - When a vehicle changes direction, forces are applied to the vehicle and its load. Braking at the same time can result in additional forces being introduced, and this can lead to a loss of control. For this reason, braking should be carried out while driving in a straight line, so preventing these forces from acting together.

Question 48

B - Local-authority environmental health departments check vehicles' exhaust emissions. They have the power to prosecute the driver and the operator, as do enforcement bodies such as DVSA.

Question 49

You're returning to the UK and are about to board a ferry. An immigration officer asks to see your documentation. What must you show them immediately?

A   Your operator documentation

B   Your vehicle registration document

C   Your driver's hours record

D   Your driving licence

Question 50

What does this sign mean?

A   Speed humps

B   Uneven road

C   Risk of grounding

D   Road liable to subsidence

Question 49

A - Operators must set up an 'effective system' to prevent the carriage of illegal immigrants. This should include documentation with advice on vehicle security and a list of checks to be made. These papers should be produced immediately if an immigration officer asks to see them.

Question 50

C - If you see this sign, be aware that there's a danger of grounding. This can happen where there's a pronounced bump in the road, such as at a level crossing or a hump bridge.

More Practise?

Become a member with UK Driving Skills and get access to around 900+ Theory Test Revision Questions, produced under licence from the DVSA.

Our interactive online tests each have 100 questions and are timed just like the real thing. You'll also be given a score at the end, plus an explanation of the answers.

Hazard Perception

We also offer packages which allow you to study for the hazard perception test with access to over 130 official practise videos.

Visit https://www.ukdrivingskills.co.uk **for more info**

Printed in Great Britain
by Amazon